HE
SENT
HIM

UNDERSTANDING and RELEASING
the power of the Holy Spirit in your life

TODD SMITH

HE SENT HIM
by Todd Smith
Copyright © 2019 Todd Smith

ISBN: 9781090704269

Cover Design: Marty Darracott

Unless otherwise indicated,
all Scripture quotations are taken from the *New King James Version*, copyright ©
Italics and bold highlights in scriptural passages are for emphasis only.

Dedication

I dedicate this book to Mike Martin, Perry Buckner, Jimmy Hope, and the wonderful pastor of the church where I received the baptism with the Holy Spirit, Buddy Barron. These men will forever hold a special place in my heart. Why? They prayed for me to receive the fullness of the Holy Spirit.

When I was in that Pentecostal church, frightened, but hungry, no one really knew how it would all end up. Well, here I am, years later, sharing my story how a group of faithful men helped a hungry young Baptist pastor experience the baptism with the Spirit.

I am forever grateful to these ministers for their patience, love and care. You share in the fruit of my ministry and this book. Only heaven will reveal the true impact you have had on the Kingdom. May God bless you!

Acknowledgments

Special thanks goes to my supportive group of elders. Their unwavering love for me and my family is cherished and has allowed me to grow as a person and a pastor. I love your heart for God and for the House of the Lord.

Also, the ministerial and support staff God has given me is second to none. They are the hardest-working people I have ever been associated with. Each of them has an insatiable passion for His presence.

To our church family at Christ Fellowship Church, Dawsonville: Years ago the Lord spoke to me and said, "Do not build Me a church of attenders, but build Me an Army that I can use."

You guys have done everything the Lord required of you, and now you are an Army of specialists. Just look how the Lord has used - and *is using* - our tribe!

To my boys! Thanks, Ty and Ethan!

You two have persevered and stayed true. Now, God is giving you both an opportunity to impact the world. Never has a dad been more proud than I am of you! Both Pops would be super proud of the men you have become!

And my wife, Karen, who has consistently contended for the truth. There is no one on the planet more in love with their Savior than she is. One day when you stand before Him, He will simply smile and say, "Well done!"

TABLE OF CONTENTS

Foreword

My heart is so stirred by the powerful new book, "He Sent Him," by my dear friend, Pastor Todd Smith.

This book will become a handbook for the desperate of heart and of spirit who simply desire to know God at a deeper level than ever before.

Todd teaches us that, through the in-filling of the Spirit, each one of us can embark on the greatest adventure we could ever imagine. This book is a clarion call for every believer who desires to go deeper in their walk with God.

You will be awakened to recognize that the entire plan of God is for you to realize THIS IS YOUR NOW!

Todd shows us that our God is "*no respecter of persons*," but that He is simply looking for vessels He can fill with His Spirit, power and authority. And Todd meticulously shows us that God is simply waiting for you to "ask, seek and knock."

His Spirit will empower you to do that.

We must allow the Holy Spirit direct access to our lives. This means that each of us must eagerly desire the Gifts of the Spirit. (1 Corinthians 14:1) We are also called to house within each of us the Holy Spirit. (1 Corinthians 3:16)

This book will show you how and why!

As you journey through this powerful book, you will be stirred to fall upon your face in order to experience exactly what the disciples experienced in the Upper Room. The Acts 2 experience was not just for a few disciples in an upper room, but it was a blue-print for the New Testament believer.

I truly believe that this book is a mandate from heaven to lead all believers into the baptism with the Holy Spirit. As an evangelist who has traveled the world, one of the greatest sights I have ever witnessed is that of believers being baptized in the fire of God. I have seen this on five different continents and in millions of lives.

Nothing compares to seeing a hungry believer receive the in-filling of God's Spirit. To see God literally change their very identity in a matter of moments is a sight to behold.

God gave us His Spirit so that we would never again feel orphaned. (John 14:18)

We must have every single weapon that God has provided. The days ahead are perilous for the believer. This is a time where you will be persecuted for your beliefs. Biblical truth is under attack by a secular culture. Yet, God has partnered with us to make His message known to the world. It is time to be bold and radical. He has anointed us for such a time as this. It is time to be separated, and counted upon, for such a high calling.

The Apostle Paul gave us this amazing instruction in 2 Corinthians 6:14–18:

"*Don't become partners with those who reject God. How can you make a partnership out of right and wrong? That's not partnership; that's war. Is light best friends with dark? Does Christ go strolling with the Devil? Do trust and mistrust hold hands?*

Who would think of setting up pagan idols in God's holy Temple? But that is exactly what we are, each of us a temple in whom God lives. God himself put it this way: 'I'll live in them, move into them; I'll be their God and they'll be my people. So leave the corruption and compromise; leave it for good,' says God. 'Don't link up with those who will pollute you. I want you all for myself. I'll be a Father to you; you'll be sons and daughters to me.' The Word of the Master, God." (The Message)

I truly believe that unless the Holy Spirit moves once again across our nation, we are doomed to destruction. I hear in my spirit the cry of 2 Chronicles 7:14: *"If my people, who are called by my name, will humble themselves and pray and seek my face and turn from their wicked ways, then I will hear from heaven, and I will forgive their sin and will heal their land."*

Therefore, it is imperative that you and I stand firm. God is looking for the bold who will take a stand for Him. He is whispering to believers, Come and drink! (Revelation 22:17)

This book is destined to be a masterpiece of prose written for the wanderer in search of more, those disenchanted with the cold, spiritless church and those hungry for more.

Thank you to my dear friend and co-revivalist, Pastor Todd Smith, for listening to Jesus to write this powerful work, titled appropriately, "HE SENT HIM."

Now it is our duty to receive HIM!

Pat Schatzline
Evangelist and author, Remnant Ministries International

1

"The Cross, The Tomb And The Upper Room"

If I told you there is more to this Christian life, would you believe me?

When I got saved, no one told me there was more. They congratulated me on my decision to follow Christ, patted me on the back, and encouraged me to be faithful to the Lord; they lovingly supported me the best way they knew how. So my journey of living for Jesus began and, at that time - and for many years - I didn't know there was more.

But *now I do*!

You see, I was living on the right side of Easter, but on the wrong side of Pentecost. Let me expound.

I fully embraced Jesus and His complete work on the cross. Because of His death and resurrection I was forgiven of my sin and became a new creation. I loved the Lord and, in the deepest part of my heart, I longed to please Him. However, my relationship with Christ only went so far. Something was missing and I didn't know what it was.

My problem was, I never entered the Upper Room for myself. I lived for Him, but I lacked power.

I believe the vast majority of Christians have had an encounter with Jesus; they have bowed their hearts to the Lord, repented of their sin and committed to follow Him, but have not been endued with power. They have been indwelled by the Spirit, but the Spirit hasn't come *upon* them.

> "The Spirit-filled life is not a special, deluxe edition of Christianity. It is part and parcel of the total plan of God for His people." A. W. Tozer

Let me explain the difference. When a person gets saved, the Holy Spirit comes to indwell them. The indwelling presence of the Spirit is for their personal benefit. He becomes their Comforter, Guide, Teacher, Helper, and Friend. (John 14-16) He will be ever present and never leave them, nor forsake them. (Hebrews 13:5)

However, the baptism with the Holy Spirit is when the Spirit of God comes "upon" an individual and empowers him or her for His service. When this sweet encounter happens, it is for the benefit of others. Jesus said, *"When the Holy Spirit comes 'upon' you, you shall be my witnesses...."* (Acts 1:8)

Here is my assessment. Far too many people in the body of Christ are living their lives huddled at the foot of the cross and at the entrance of the tomb. That is the way I was.

I know that sounds heretical. Believe me, I don't mean for it to be. I am not minimizing these two beautiful encounters and experiences. They are the foundation of the gospel, and without them, we have no "good news." However, many Christians, by default, stop there and don't move forward. The Holy Spirit indwells them, but they haven't yet marched to the Upper Room.

For multiple reason(s), people have pitched their tents between the cross and the Upper Room.

This means they have experienced the new birth and the wonderful benefits in the resurrection of Jesus, but have yet to encounter the full power of Pentecost.

So, for many, their Christian walk is lacking the necessary power in order to execute His will on the earth. Being saved, for them, has become about "surviving," "hanging on" and "making it" to the end.

That is not what God intended.

I was raised as a Southern Baptist and I constantly heard messages about the cross, the atonement, the love of God, the blood of Jesus, the forgiveness of sin, redemption, becoming a new creation and getting to heaven. These messages affirmed in me the fact that I was "good and saved," and today I have a great understanding of the value and purpose of the atoning death of Jesus.

17

However, my mentors never took me to the Upper Room and introduced me to the power and purpose of Pentecost.

WARNING: I think you need to brace yourself before you read the next line.

God never intended for Christianity to end at the cross. Christ's death, burial and resurrection are the beginning place, where we receive the forgiveness of sin and become born again. It is step one, the launching pad.

There is more: the **Spirit-*filled*** life.

A. W. Tozer said it best, "The Spirit-filled life is not a special, deluxe edition of Christianity. It is part and parcel of the total plan of God for His people."

Again, there is a huge difference between being "indwelled" by the Spirit and being "empowered" by the Spirit.

If it weren't so, Jesus would not have given the disciples the mandate to go to Jerusalem in order to be "endued" with power by the Spirit. (Luke 24:49)

Furthermore, after Jesus' triumph over death, He didn't say to His disciples, "Let's go back to the top of the hill where they crucified Me," nor, "Let's visit the tomb where they buried me."

No, after He appeared to His disciples, His command was direct and clear: "Get to Jerusalem, find your way to a room on the top floor and don't leave until you are baptized with the Holy Spirit." (Acts 1:4, 12, 13)

Neither would Jesus – if He had intended for us to only be *indwelled* by the Spirit – have instructed Ananias to go to

Saul (Paul) and lay hands on him so he could receive the power of the Spirit. (Acts 9:17)

Jesus pushed His disciples to the Upper Room. In fact, He commanded them to go there. He refused to let them remain at Golgotha or the empty tomb.

He required more!

He commanded them to go to Jerusalem and wait until they were endued with power.

The same is true for us. He wants us to realize there is another stop, another place to visit. I am so thankful I discovered it.

Your personal experience with the fullness of the Holy Spirit is the single most significant event that you will ever have as a Christian. If one fails to have this encounter he/she will fall short of God's plan for their lives. Jesus made it abundantly clear that the baptism with the Holy Spirit was priority number one for His followers; and 2,000 years later it hasn't changed.

Wouldn't it be a terrible moment, on the day you stand before God, if He revealed to you that He had more for you that you had never experienced?

It would be a travesty to know you had an opportunity to encounter more of Him and *didn't*!

In the pages that follow, you will discover what the "more" is and what the fuss is all about. As you read, prepare yourself for a bumpy ride.

You are gonna laugh, cry, question, doubt and - oh yeah! - be challenged. My ultimate quest is to get you up the stairs to the Upper Room to encounter **the more**.

2

Running Out Of Gas

One New Years Day some years ago, during the Tournament of Roses parade, a dazzling colorful float suddenly sputtered and quit—it was out of gas. Oh the horror! Can you imagine the chaos that ensued? The one thing you thought could never happen *happened*. The whole parade was held up until someone could run and get a can of gas and refuel the flowered car.

You might be wondering how this could happen on such a big stage. How could this significant detail get overlooked? Certainly somebody was responsible for checking the gas gauge. It is intriguing to note who the sponsor of this float was. Are you ready for the answer? The Standard Oil Company! That's right! This beautiful float was representing one of the biggest gasoline producers in the world, and it ran out of gas.

Before I judge the oil company too harshly, I remember back in the day, when I first started driving, my gas tank was rusty just above the two-dollar mark. Some of you know what I'm talking about. It seemed all I ever had was two dollars worth of gas to put into my tank.

While driving, like most responsible people, I closely monitored the gas gauge. I looked at it often, and I quickly learned that "E" didn't really mean empty; it meant "*almost* empty." I knew exactly how many more miles I had when the needle was completely on the E.

Truthfully, I lived on the edge when it came to "gas in the tank." Being a veteran of this sort of thing, when and if things got touch and go - I had a well-thought-out plan. It came in phases, and step one was called, "Contingency Plan One."

First, I would turn the radio off. Why? I really don't know, but I did. Second, the air conditioner was switched off, minimizing the work load and power demand of the engine. Third, I rolled up all the windows. (Notice that I said "rolled up" the windows; I didn't have electric windows.) I had to reduce wind drag, thus becoming more aerodynamic. Never mind that I would be sweating to death; I was in survival mode. I had to do what needed to be done.

Next, when possible, I would throw the car into neutral and coast as far as I could, thereby preserving every drop of gas.

I have to confess, on more than one occasion I grossly miscalculated. Perhaps it was my angle when viewing the gas needle. Frankly, there is no worse feeling than when your car begins to sputter, cough and shake. When it does, it is sending you the horrifying message, "the end is near."

On cue, your blood sprints to your feet, you break out into a cold sweat, you have difficulty breathing; plus, you see your loved ones flash before your eyes. Then the worst thing happens: you see your mom's all-knowing, loving face and hear her last words to you as you left the house, "Hey Babe, here's two dollars. Be sure to stop and get some gas."

Then you snap out of it because you know you only have seconds to respond to your car's death rattle.

Experienced "out-of-gas" people realize at this moment in the process that you don't have time to panic, so you methodically - like it's your second nature - transition into the next phase: "Contingency Plan Two."

Immediately after the first failed gulp your engine takes for more gas you begin to swerve and swing the car from side to side. Yep, you weave from line to line. Why? You want to get the tiny bit of gas at the bottom of your tank to splash over to where the gas line is in order to get the last few ounces of gas to the engine. This is a precise practice.

A person who is a novice at running out of gas doesn't understand the delicate nuances of such maneuvering. The timing of the swerving and momentum shifts are paramount.

I may have failed Geometry in High School, but I was a Rocket Scientist when it came to gas displacement. I must add, this advanced skill-set is acquired over time and in on-the-job training. Sadly, I know all about it and have a black belt in swerving. I quickly learned if you pivot well and navigate the remaining morsel of gas to the gas line, it will allow you a few extra minutes to get to a gas station.

Embarrassingly, I can recall a time or two (or three) when I did run out of gas. These were pre-cell-phone days and if you ran out of gas, you were on your own. You couldn't text daddy to come to your rescue while you waited on the side

23

of the road. No, you had to endure the walk of shame all the way to a total stranger's house.

How about you? Have you had the fearful experience of running out of gas?

If you're like me, you can recall the ordeal as if it were yesterday, as it is forever etched into the grey matter of the brain. Here is what often transpires.

As you step on the porch, you muster all the dignity you have left and, with your chin high, you timidly knock on the front door. Deep down, you are praying to the good Lord that Freddy Krueger or one of his distant cousins doesn't come to the door wearing a ski mask. All of your senses are heightened, especially your ears. You are listening for the banjo music.

After a few attempts you finally hear the approaching footsteps. The homeowner cautiously cracks open the door as one eye scans your entire frame. For a brief moment, you feel subhuman, inferior, violated, and completely unworthy of bearing the last name of your father. Your next step is to explain to him why you are on his front porch. This is where you humbly ask, "I'm sorry, but I ran out of gas down the road a piece. May I borrow some gas?"

He opens the door wider and every time, without fail, he says, "Yes."

Then the march happens; you know, where you walk a couple of paces behind the homeowner with your shoulders slumped and your head down. You dare not look up. He leads the way to the shed to fetch the red gas can. It's on the shelf next to the rusty grey metal tool box. He extends it to you and all he says is, "Here ya go." You give a quick glance into his eyes, and respectfully say, "Thanks, I'll bring it right back."

You slowly turn and walk back to your car. You quickly, but carefully empty all of the gas from the borrowed can, every single drop. Nothing is wasted. And life returns to normal.

Are You Out Of Gas?

Spiritually speaking, how many of us are attempting to live the Christian life the same way we drove our cars? Running on empty, or worse, running on fumes? Without a doubt, some of us, if we are honest, are physically and spiritually completely out of gas.

This is not God's best for our life. God knew we couldn't make Christianity work on our own. Therefore, He supplied us with the necessary fuel in the Person of the Holy Spirit.

The Holy Spirit is the "gasoline" that gives us power to live for Him and to do His will on the earth. Too many of us are unnecessarily exhausted, depleted and defeated. Basically we have little to no energy left, nor strength to effectively do His work. We are doing the best we can, trying to make things happen for ourselves and God, but we are missing His power.

Jesus knew "running out of gas" would be a huge problem for His first followers, so He instructed His disciples to go to Jerusalem and wait to be "filled" with His Spirit.

Jesus told them, *"...you shall receive POWER when the Holy Spirit comes upon you."* (Acts 1:8)

He also knew that "running out of gas" would be a problem for us as well. Therefore, throughout the New Testament He commands us, His children, to be "filled with the Spirit." He promised us that He would fill our tank so we have the strength and power to live for Him.

Right now I would like for you to take a look at the spiritual "gas needle" of your life. Where is it? What does it reveal? Is your tank half empty or, like the majority, is the needle on E?

I have some great news for you! It doesn't have to remain there. God has made provision for you to experience His wonderful Spirit.

I promise you this: if you will let Him, He will fill your tank to overflowing, or way above the two-dollar mark!

"Blessed are those who hunger and thirst for righteousness, for they shall be filled." (Matthew 5:6)

3

When God Exhales

A sweet lady in her mid-eighties was quietly sitting in a waiting room preparing to see her doctor. Across from her, two friends were discussing life and the church one of them pastored. The older lady, who appeared to be looking at her magazine, was snooping and listening in on their apparently private conversation.

When she discovered that one of them was a pastor, she took liberty and interrupted their discussion. The two were somewhat surprised by the stark interruption from the unexpected intruder. (I guess you can do anything you want when you are 85.) She blurted, "You know what you need to preach on?" as she dropped the magazine to her lap.

27

"Breath! Without it you don't have anything." She went on to explain that she had asthma and was having a hard time getting it under control. Her inability to breathe taught her the value of breath.

Our bodies are fearfully and wonderfully made by God and even the smallest of details still intrigues the greatest medical and scientific minds of our time. The human body is quite a complex machine. For example, the body can go nearly two months without food and several days without water and still remain alive. However, the body can only live 4-8 minutes without getting a breath of air.

Research indicates we take an average of sixteen breaths per minute. Do the math: that is 23,040 breaths a day, 8,409,600 in a year and if you live to be 75 you would have inhaled and exhaled 630,720,000 times. That is a lot of breathing!

"Breath! Without it you don't have anything."

God breathes. In the beginning, it was His breath that created. He breathed on mankind and gave him His life. He continued to breathe on people, places, situations, and gatherings as we see throughout the scriptures.

In Genesis 1, we see the initial effect of the breath of God as He exhaled upon the earth. In this passage, the world - before the touch of His breath - was empty and dark. The writer used words such as void, dark, deep, and without form. The text conveys the idea that the unformed world was chaotic, lifeless, and out of control. But with one gust of His breath, all creation was commanded into order.

"The earth was without form, and void; and darkness was on the face of the deep. And the Spirit of God [ruach ha kadesh] was hovering over the face of the waters." (Genesis 1:2)

In the second verse of the Bible, only twenty-nine words in, we get a significant revelation regarding the Spirit of God. The Hebrew word for Spirit used in this verse is *"Ruach"* which literally means "breath and/or wind."

The earth was just moments away from being birthed and the Spirit of God (breath of God, *"ruach ha kadesh"*) was strategically positioned *"hovering over the face of the waters."* This means the Spirit was fluttering, brooding, and trembling over the deep as if anticipating its command to action like a runner at the starting line. The undeveloped, chaotic mass we would eventually call earth was without form, unstructured and lying beneath unsettled waters. And when God said, *"let there be…,"* the breath of God immediately moved upon the deep with a ferociousness that brought form and order to the troubled darkness. Without hesitation, both darkness and chaos surrendered their will to the breath of God and the earth was formed.

29

The power in the breath of God was demonstrated in creation as His breath gave meaning to nothingness, shape to emptiness, and fullness to a place that was void and cold. Ultimately, it was His breath that brought Adam into being and caused him to walk in the garden in fellowship with God.

"Breath! Without it you don't have anything."

The Kiss Of Life

When someone stops breathing, every second matters. Life literally hangs in the balance. It is imperative that somebody step forward and perform an emergency lifesaving procedure called Cardiopulmonary Resuscitation, better known as CPR, "The Kiss of Life." Doctors tell us immediate CPR can double or triple someone's chance of survival.

There it was, the first human body, masterfully crafted, fully developed and beautiful. Nothing else compared to it; the apex of creation, a perfect man. And there was God, gazing down upon His masterpiece as it just laid there, a form, a lifeless body. No motion, nothing; all was quiet and still.

I can only speculate, but I assume all of creation at this moment was perfectly still, looking to see what God would do next. Up to this point, everything God created immediately came alive and needed nothing. However, man was different. God formed and created Adam from dirt. After God's masterful touch and perfect sculpting, his body just "existed." It was an empty shell, motionless and lifeless.

God's creation of the human body was flawless in every way. However, it lacked one thing: Breath.

God leaned forward and His face approached the face of Adam. Then it happened. He was centimeters away from Adam's nose and lips when God inhaled, and then He blew His life into Adam's nostrils. As Adam's chest cavity swelled with God's breath, Adam instantly became a living soul. God gave Adam "The Kiss of Life."

*"And the Lord God formed man of the dust of the ground, and **breathed into his nostrils** the breath of life; and man became a living being." (Genesis 2:7)*

"Breath! Without it you don't have anything."

Can These Bones Live?

King Nebuchadnezzar of the Babylonian Empire defeated Israel, deposed their king and destroyed the Temple in Jerusalem. It was a devastating time for Israel. They were mortified and hope was lost as the chosen people of God were scattered and/or placed in exile in Babylon.

Because of the tragic events that unfolded, Ezekiel the prophet was taken into a valley by the Spirit of God. For a moment the Lord allowed Ezekiel to look over the great expanse to get a true glimpse of the heart and soul of Israel.

What did Ezekiel observe in the valley?

He saw a disturbing image, a valley of chalk-like bones that were intermingled. They were everywhere, lifeless and very dry. Ezekiel knew these bones represented the dead nation of Israel and it grieved him greatly.

God broke the silence and interjected a probing question to Ezekiel (Ezekiel 37:3):

"...'Son of man, can these bones live?'"

Ezekiel responded, *"O Lord God, You know."*

God quickly instructed Ezekiel to take action and prophesy to the bones.

"Prophesy to these bones, and say to them, 'O dry bones, hear the word of the Lord!'" (Ezekiel 37:4)

"Thus says the Lord God to these bones: 'Surely I will cause breath to enter into you, and you shall live. I will put sinews on you and bring flesh upon you, cover you with skin and put breath in you; and you shall live. Then you shall know that I am the Lord.'" (Ezekiel 37:5, 6)

*"Also He said to me, **'Prophesy to the breath**, prophesy, son of man, and say to the breath, Thus says the Lord God: **'Come from the four winds, O breath, and breathe on these slain, that they may live.'"** (Ezekiel 37:9)*

*"So I prophesied as He commanded me, **and breath came into them, and they lived, and stood upon their feet, an exceedingly great army.**"* (Ezekiel 37:10)

Ezekiel did exactly as God instructed. As Ezekiel prophesied, suddenly the dry bones lying still on the desert floor started moving and flying around, looking for their matches. A beautiful scene unfolded before his eyes as the bones began connecting together. And before long, surrounding Ezekiel on every side was a great army of skeletons. That's right, skeletons!

Next, as the scripture promised, tendons, muscles, and skin covered the skeletons. (v. 6) While Ezekiel prophesied, the bones became draped in flesh. As this miracle occurred Ezekiel became encircled by corpses, non-breathing bodies. They had flesh, a heart, a brain, the necessary organs and even blood in their veins, but they were still lifeless.

Their condition was similar to Adam in the Garden of Eden, a body fully developed but with no breath.

The story didn't end there. Ezekiel prophesied one more time. He commanded that the breath of God would come from the four winds of the earth and fill these cold lifeless bodies. At that precise moment, the **breath of God** came and filled each corpse with His life; the bodies instantly stood up on their feet!

*"...and breath came into them, **and they lived, and stood upon their feet**, an exceedingly great army."*

The breath of God enabled these dead bodies to stand up!

"Breath! Without it you don't have anything."

God Breathed On Them

There they were, just a handful of Jesus' disciples trying to make sense as to what happened over the last few days.

One minute they were having dinner with their beloved Rabbi; the next, they followed Him to a place of sweet solitude to pray, and suddenly, out of nowhere Jesus was surrounded by soldiers and arrested. Within sixteen hours He was nailed to a cross and declared dead.

Three days later, the word around town was, *He is alive!*

Some of His disciples were locked away in a secluded place hiding from the Jews. (John 20:19) Perhaps unsure of where to go and to whom they could turn, they felt alone, abandoned, afraid and understandably angry. No doubt they were rehearsing the events that transpired over the last several days. Then it happened.

Jesus walked into the room. He didn't even knock, or bother to walk through the doorway. No, He just appeared. Out of thin air, boom, there He was!

In John 20:21-22, we see that *"Jesus said to them again, 'Peace to you! As the Father has sent Me, I also send you.' And when He had said this, He breathed on them, and said to them, 'Receive the Holy Spirit.'"*

Make sure you fully grasp what took place. Jesus came in the room unannounced and completely interrupted their small gathering. He proceeded to make a few statements, reminding them of their assignment, and, without warning, He suddenly emptied all the air in His lungs as He blew on them.

Can you see it? Jesus took in a deep breath, and then He exhaled on His disciples. We are not told what happened to them or what reaction they had, but one can only imagine how they responded when they felt the breath of God on their face and as their lungs filled with His breath.

Jesus commanded His disciples to go to the Upper Room and wait until they were endued with power.

"Breath! Without it you don't have anything."

Jesus breathing on His disciples was, for them, just a foretaste of what was about to occur in their lives. Jesus commanded His disciples to go to the Upper Room and wait until they were endued with power. They were ordered to wait on His breath, His Spirit. And, in obedience to the Lord's instruction, they went and tarried. The Bible says, as they were praying, the sound of a **mighty rushing wind filled the room**. (Acts 2:2)

From heaven, the Lord exhaled His breath upon the one hundred twenty disciples who were gathered in the Upper Room. Immediately they received strength and power to become His witnesses. From that point, they began to lay hands on the sick, cast out devils and cure diseases, just as He taught them to do.

His breath gave them power and life!

35

I am reminded of the eighty-five year old lady in the waiting room, and her exhortation:

"Breath! Without it you
don't have anything."

4

Let
The Fire
Fall

For decades, these exact words could be heard from the base of Glacier Point Mountain as spectators gathered by the hundreds to watch fire fall from the top.

"Let the fire fall!" they cried.

Visitors who traveled to the picturesque Curry Village in Yosemite National Park were highly encouraged to come back later in the evening to see an event they would never forget.

In 1872, a breathtaking tradition was started by James McCauley, owner of the Glacier Point Mountain House Hotel.

During the daytime the McCauleys would gather wood and debris and make the hottest and largest fire possible on top of the mountain. This would go on for hours with them adding more wood, for more fire.

As daylight surrendered to darkness the campers and tourists quickly gathered for the event. Many relaxed comfortably in lawn chairs while others sat on blankets strewn on the ground. All of them, young and old, anxiously waited for the fire to fall from the sky.

Each and every summer night, exactly at 9 PM, a Park Ranger at the top of the mountain would shout as loud as he could to the spectators below, *"Are you ready, Camp Curry?"*

When a Park Ranger at the base of the mountain, who basically acted as a master of ceremonies, heard the thunderous question he would quickly survey the hopeful, energetic crowd. After observing their impressive excitement he would cup his hands around his mouth and yell back as loud as possible to the Park Ranger up on the mountain, **"WE ... ARE ... READY! LET THE FIRE FALL!"**

At that moment the red-hot glowing embers were pushed over the ledge of Glacier Point Mountain, resulting in a suddenly blazing fire free-falling 3,000 feet to the canyon floor, creating a literal, glittering "Waterfall of Fire."

Understandably, the crowd below was mesmerized and astounded as fire cascaded from the sky. The scene was spectacular. Each evening they would burst out in applause as the last ember reached the valley floor. Even though the event only lasted seconds, it left a lasting impression on all who experienced it.

Throughout the years this became one of Yosemite National Park's most famous spectacles: The Yosemite Firefall. This incredible event continued for almost a hundred years. Unfortunately, in 1968, George Hertzog, the director of the National Park Service, decided to end the Yosemite Firefall once and for all. He stated that the Firefall was an unnatural spectacle more appropriate for Disneyland than a national park.[1]

How sad that fire no longer falls from the top of that beautiful mountain!

I have a strong conviction that what happened on top of Glacier Point Mountain is currently happening in heaven. The fire is burning and the embers are red-hot and ready. Heaven is ready to send the fire.

Let us not forget what John the Baptist said about Jesus:

*"I indeed baptize you with water unto repentance, but He who is coming after me is mightier than I, whose sandals I am not worthy to carry. **He will baptize you with the Holy Spirit and fire**."* (Matthew 3:11)

At this exact moment Jesus is leaning forward and looking at our precious churches, wonderful pastors, leaders, and all of His beloved children and He is shouting from heaven,

"Are you ready for the fire to fall?"

How will we respond? What will be our reaction?

---

[1] Yosemite Firefall, https://yosemitefirefall.com/yosemite-firefall-glacier-point/

Let's be like the Park Ranger at the base of the mountain, and cup our hands to our mouths and yell back to Him,

"We...Are...Ready! Let The Fire Fall!"

5

He Came At 9 AM

A friendly-faced little boy was in a giant mall standing alone at the base of an escalator. An observant and concerned saleslady asked, "Son, are you lost?"

"No, ma'am. I'm waiting for my chewing gum to come back."

Dare, if you will, for a moment, put yourself in this little man's shoes. Everything in his known world has come to a screeching stop. Can you imagine the excruciating agony this poor fellow experienced? One moment his taste buds were singing the Hallelujah Chorus and then before he knew it, the gum leapt out of his mouth onto a moving silver dragon, and he watched helplessly as it was steadily whisked away.

He had to be distraught and heartbroken. However, he was not going to be undone. He wasn't going to let the escalator monster get away with it. He, like most children, knew the escalator's game; he understood his gum would eventually come back around; but when?

I can see him now leaning forward with his eyeballs fixed on every passing step, scanning the grooves as others stepped around him and onto the escalator for their ride up to the second level. All the while, he was anticipating the moment he could reach down, reclaim his gum and, obviously, insert it into his mouth again.

I love the quote by the twenty-eighth President of the United States, Woodrow Wilson: "All things come to him who waits - provided he knows what he is waiting for."

The sweet young boy knew exactly what he was waiting for - his gum. Jesus' disciples also knew what they were waiting for.

In obedience to Jesus' instruction to remain in Jerusalem, one hundred twenty of His closest followers found themselves in the Upper Room - you guessed it - WAITING! Just like the little boy at the escalator, they were standing by, needing something to happen.

What were they expecting to happen? They were waiting for Jesus to fulfill the promise He made to them: that they would receive the baptism with the Holy Spirit, a baptism of power and fire!

But when?

Let's not forget, fifty-three days earlier Jesus was brutally beaten and publicly nailed to a cross. What did the disciples do?

But above it all, one hundred twenty of Jesus' closest friends were patiently waiting to experience a baptism of fire - a baptism that would propel them back into the same city, to the same people that ruthlessly killed their Leader.

The disciples, scared and confused, all scattered to find a safe place of hiding. They watched from a comfortable distance as their Lord was publicly scourged, "tried" and crucified.

Now, a short seven and a half weeks later, they found themselves in the heart of Jerusalem on the top floor of a rustic old building. All doors and windows were open; the sun shot forth a soft brisk light as the cool morning breeze filled the room. The aromas from early morning baking were undeniable and pleasurable. And the chatter between sellers and buyers from the market below brought a sense of purpose and perspective.

But above it all, one hundred twenty of Jesus' closest friends were patiently waiting to experience a baptism of fire - a baptism that would propel them back into the same city, to the same people that ruthlessly killed their Leader.

Every day in the room, the activities and routine were the same; they assembled in unity, talked among themselves, prayed and worshiped God, all while waiting for the promise. Nine days came and went and then came the appointed day.

*"Then they returned to Jerusalem from the mount called Olivet, which is near Jerusalem, a Sabbath day's journey. And when they had entered, **they went up into the upper room where they were staying... These all continued with one accord in prayer and supplication**, with the women and Mary the mother of Jesus, and with His brothers." (Acts 1:12-14)*

I'm sure they were wondering, "What's taking so long? The last nine days ended the same: nothing, no baptism of fire."

Then it happened! Jesus delivered on His promise.

*"When the Day of Pentecost had fully come, they were all with one accord in one place. And suddenly there came a sound from heaven, as of a rushing mighty wind, and it filled the **whole house** where they were sitting. Then there appeared to them divided tongues, as of fire, and one sat upon each of them. And **they were all filled with the Holy Spirit** and began to speak with other tongues, as the Spirit gave them utterance." (2:1-4)*

At 9:00 in the morning, the Holy Spirit blasted into the room like a Category 4 hurricane. (Acts 2:15)

Not one disciple could have expected it to be this way. This event was distinctly different than anything they had ever experienced. They had no frame of reference for what just happened, nothing more than a promise that they would receive power from on high and it would enable them to be His witnesses. That's it, just a command to wait for power.

The Bible implies the **whole HOUSE** experienced the jolting impact of God's Spirit as they were baptized with the **Holy Spirit and fire**.

When the Holy Spirit came to the top floor, nothing in the room remained the same. Everything shook! Naturally speaking, I believe the raw suddenness and force by which the Holy Spirit came actually alarmed the disciples.

The Bible says *"**suddenly** there came...."* The word "suddenly" comes from the Greek word *aphno*, which carries with it the idea that something happened unexpectedly, and by surprise. In other words, it happened without warning.

Even though they were "looking forward" to the Holy Spirit's baptism, He came abruptly and caught the disciples completely off guard.

In addition, Acts 2:2 says there was a **"sound"** that filled the room.

The word **"sound"** is the Greek word *echos*. This is the exact word that Luke used to describe the deafening roar of the sea. (Luke 21:5)

Again, can you imagine the response? Out of nowhere came an ear-piercing sound that echoed off the interior walls of the Upper Room.

Work with me here. Place yourself in their shoes. This is the tenth day that you have gathered with some of your best buddies. You are in a room praying and worshiping God with one hundred twenty others. Everything is relatively quiet, and then, out of nowhere, without warning, you hear a sound - not just any sound, but a *thundering* sound!

According to the text, that sound originated from heaven, the throne room of God, as if it was a rushing mighty wind. This is interesting on many fronts.

*"And suddenly there came a sound from heaven, as of a rushing mighty wind, and it filled the **whole house** where they were sitting." (Acts 2:2)*

The word **"rushing"** comes from the Greek word *phero*, which means to be moved, a gust of wind, or driven with force or speed. When this sound occurred, it was so loud and forceful that Luke classified it as a "rushing."

Luke also said it was a "mighty" rushing wind. Why is this interesting? The Greek word used is *biaios* and it translates as violent. No, the Holy Spirit wasn't violent on that day, but it does denote a fierceness about the Spirit's intent.

It gets better…

The word "wind" comes from *pnoe*. Not just wind like a flowing gentle breeze, but the sound of a violent, mighty, boisterous wind.

What does all of this mean?

One thing we know for sure, right before the disciples' eyes, in a nanosecond, the Church was birthed and introduced to the world in an unrefined manner and with an unapologetic explosion of power.

No, it was anything but quaint, reverent and gentle. On the contrary, it was loud, noisy, overpowering and relentless.

In addition, this means when the Spirit was poured out it wasn't done quietly. No, it was anything but quaint, reverent and gentle. On the contrary, it was loud, noisy, overpowering and relentless.

Why such an extravagant display? Why was the Spirit so ferocious in His manifestation?

Jesus knew His disciples were about to embark on the mission to tell the world the gospel story. In their current state, they had no heavenly power and would be unable to stand up to the religious opposition and demonic forces that awaited them. They needed power to be able to represent Him well and to fulfill the Great Commission.

Just like the early disciples, each of us needs His power. Without it we will struggle to walk in victory and will be unable to fulfill the purpose God has for us.

The good news is, **you can experience everything the first disciples did**! The same encounter they had, you can have!

Isn't that amazing?

Don't forget, we have the same mandate they had; therefore, we need the same power they had. And the pathway to have the power they had is to have the same experience they had.

We need an Upper Room experience of our own!

I have learned that for the Christian, the baptism with the Holy Spirit is the most significant encounter a believer can have. It isn't only important; it is a NECESSITY!

God's will is for each of you to have this blessed experience.

The following pages will chronicle my journey and how the Holy Spirit filled this Southern Baptist pastor.

HE CAME AT 9!

6

A Southern Baptist Pastor Encounters The Holy Spirit

On July 4, 1776, history doesn't record any event of particular value occurred in England. It was just a typical day, without any fanfare.

However, across the ocean on that same day, members of the Continental Congress meeting in a smoke-filled room in Philadelphia signed a document that would ignite the American Revolution, birth a nation and, eventually, change the world.

That's a lot like the way my revolution began.

To some it was just another Thursday in September. Yes, it was a beautiful fall day, just like many others before it, but on this particular day my life, ministry, family and future were forever changed by an encounter with the power of God.

It was around 11 in the morning and I, an ordained Southern Baptist pastor, found myself surrounded by four spirit-filled, blood-bought, tongue-talking Pentecostals. Boy, I was in trouble and I knew it. Being a good Southern Baptist, deep down I recognized I was in the wrong place with the wrong people. According to some, I was committing high treason.

You have to know, I received degrees of higher learning from two of the finest Southern Baptist institutions, Samford University in Birmingham, Alabama, and Southwestern Baptist Theological Seminary in Fort Worth, Texas. Furthermore, I was born a Southern Baptist, raised as a Southern Baptist, saved, baptized and called into the ministry as a Southern Baptist. This is all I had ever known; this was my religious identity. I also served for nine and a half years on the ministerial staffs at Southern Baptist churches. Therefore, my meeting with these Spirit-filled Pentecostals was never supposed to happen.

Oddly enough, I had never been to a Pentecostal prayer meeting. (I had one brief encounter with Pentecostalism as a teen - which I'll address later - but what I experienced there was not enough to ease my mind on this day.) I was as nervous as a cat in a room full of rocking chairs. I've got to be honest, I was more than nervous, I was scared to death! Think about it - a Baptist boy at a Pentecostal prayer meeting! A recipe for disaster, right?

On the exterior, the twenty-five-minute drive to the prayer meeting was quiet and uneventful. However, a thousand different thoughts raced through my anxious mind.

After arriving at the church, I stayed in the car for a bit to collect my thoughts. Within a few minutes, I emerged and, as I closed the car door behind me, I took a deep breath and marched nervously toward the entrance of the church. As my feet crossed the threshold I thought, "Oh my, what have I gotten myself into?"

I truly didn't know what to expect. My eyes and ears were wide open. Even though I was a little afraid and tentative, my hunger for God kept me in the room. I went to this prayer meeting determined, and I was there for one purpose: to experience the baptism with the Holy Spirit.

How Did It Come To This?

My quest for the fullness of God started innocently enough. During quiet moments, I began to question if there was more of God than what I was currently experiencing. Deep down I felt there was more, that there *had* to be more.

There were several reasons I began to ask that question. I will only mention four them.

1. Even though I was a "successful pastor," I knew I was missing something.

Even though I was a little afraid and tentative, my hunger for God kept me in the room.

51

What made this so unusual was that the church I was pastoring was flourishing. All the exterior indicators pointed out that I should have been more than satisfied. Additional staff members were being added, a new sanctuary was being built, and lots of people were being saved.

In fact, when it came to baptisms, our church was consistently in the top 40 of the Southern Baptist churches in the state of Georgia. You must realize, at that time there were over 3,000 Southern Baptist churches in the state.

My own walk with God was fresh and thriving. On the surface everything was fine. However, way down deep in the core of my soul I knew something was not right, something was missing. While enjoying the benefits of being a pastor of a growing church, I was experiencing emptiness on the inside. This void was getting deeper with each passing day. Regardless of how much I studied the word of God, prayed and worshiped, this vacuum would not go away.

2. I started watching TBN (Trinity Broadcasting Network) with an open mind.

Before my encounter with the Holy Spirit, I would make fun of and ridicule what I saw on TBN broadcasts. However, the more I watched, the more intrigued I became. I started noticing that the special guests on their programs were different than me. I knew I was just as saved as they were, yet they seemed to possess a power, an anointing and a joy that I did not have. The more I watched, the clearer it became. I kept hearing minister after minister talk about "the baptism with the Holy Spirit," a term that I didn't fully understand.

Sadly, during my ministry at my Baptist church I discouraged my friends and church members from investigating or even discussing the baptism with the Holy Spirit. As far as I was concerned, that doctrine was erroneous and heretical. However, the more I watched TBN, the more I heard well-educated, successful Pentecostal ministers talk about the baptism with the Holy Spirit. This was the first time in my life I truly stopped and, with an open mind, listened to their point of view. In the past, I was critical and judgmental of such people. On many occasions I mocked such teaching.

The more I watched, the more troubled I became.

I pondered in my spirit night after night, "What if they are right and I am wrong? What if the baptism with the Holy Spirit is real?" I could not escape these probing questions; they continuously echoed in the back of my mind.

3. I compared my ministry with the ministry of the early disciples in the book of Acts.

In my private reading of the Bible, especially the book of Acts, I would read the startling accounts of the crippled walking, the blind seeing, the mute speaking, the dead being raised and the demonized being set free. I quickly came to the sobering realization that, despite the success of my ministry, it was a far cry from what Peter and Paul demonstrated in the book of Acts. They obviously had a power working in them that I did not have.

What made the difference?

Answering that question became my constant obsession as the Father was gently revealing to me my lack of spiritual power.

4. In the midst of my search I received a phone call

My friend was home on furlough after serving in Singapore as a missionary. His phone call was unexpected; it had been several years since we last talked. We attended Southwestern Baptist Theological Seminary together in Fort Worth, Texas. To me, he was the quintessential Southern Baptist, so the conversation that followed surprised me. Honestly, it shocked me.

There was very little small talk, he jumped right in and started sharing with me what was taking place in his ministry on the mission field. He calmly mentioned how the power of God was in demonstration in his life and church. Then, without reservation he told me how he had entered into a deeper walk with God. Immediately, he had my attention. I pressed the phone tighter to my ear; my breathing slowed down; I wanted to hear every word. He shared openly about the signs and wonders that were taking place in his ministry and church.

"This was not the same guy I went to seminary with; something was different, way different."

I thought to myself, "This was not the same guy I went to seminary with; something was different, way different." The more he talked, the more excited I became. I couldn't believe that someone I knew intimately and trusted had experienced what I was craving.

In the middle of our conversation, I came right out and asked him, "Steve, do you speak in tongues?" That was the only way I knew to express myself, the only question I knew to ask.

To my surprise He responded, "Yes!"

I was alarmed by his response. Then he added, "It's not just about speaking in tongues, it's about experiencing the fullness of God and His power."

I interrupted him and shared my pursuit and quest to discover the fullness of God's power. I asked him numerous questions about his experience and the Holy Spirit. He patiently answered all of them and then he emphatically told me that the baptism with the Holy Spirit was real and that it changed his life.

At that precise moment I knew what I needed: THE BAPTISM WITH THE HOLY SPIRIT!

After my conversation with my friend, I aggressively researched the relevance and necessity of Holy Spirit baptism. I took the time to interview several Pentecostal preachers. I asked tough, probing questions. I wanted to know what they believed and why they believed it. Don't forget, I preached and taught against this scriptural baptism and speaking in tongues, so, as a good dispensationalist, I knew all the right questions to ask.

In addition, I read books and articles, and listened to numerous teachings on the topic. I was determined to find the whole truth regarding the subject. I was not interested in denominational truth or half-truths - I wanted facts. I didn't want political, denominational talking points. I wanted to know what the Bible had to say.

Shortly after my journey began, I inadvertently realized there was a slight issue. I quickly discovered that when I would read the Bible I read it from my denominational perspective, my Baptist perspective. Here is how I realized I had a problem. On more than one occasion after reading a passage on the Holy Spirit I can distinctly remember saying to myself, "We don't believe that...." or, "...that's not for us," or, "...that was for then and not now."

I don't think I am the only one who has struggled with this. Without a doubt, many read the Word through the lens of their upbringing, Bible teaching and experiences, whether it be Baptist, Methodist or even Pentecostal. I concluded that, in order for me to clearly see and understand what the scriptures had to say about the precious baptism with Holy Spirit, I had to take off my denominational glasses.

At first that was difficult to do. These glasses meant a lot to me and I spent a lot of money buying and perfecting those lenses. I had great teachers, mentors and pastors who polished those lenses.

Furthermore, most of my friends and family had similar glasses. We all matched. However, during my investigative stage into the baptism with the Holy Spirit, I truly wanted to read the Bible without any presuppositions or built-in bias. I desired to read the Word without any filters, so the glasses had to be set aside.

Something marvelous happened when I took off my denominational glasses. The New Testament came alive to me. Scriptures and promises leapt off the page and landed in the center of my thirsty soul. I became so in love with the Word. It was as if I was reading the Bible for the very first time and I started seeing things in the Bible that I had never seen before, even though I had read the same passages numerous times. My faith and hunger for Him increased!

In addition, there was such freedom in my Bible study; I wasn't on the defensive as I read certain passages, and I didn't have to make "excuses" for why I couldn't believe particular texts. I didn't have to "explain away" what some would call controversial scriptures. And my favorite benefit? I didn't have to dodge and stay clear of certain chapters of the New Testament, nothing was "off limits." (My Baptist preacher friends know what I mean.) I read them all with joy and I had a new childlike longing to experience all of them to the fullest.

I Decided It Was Real

After more than a year of copious research, I came to the conclusion that the baptism with the Holy Spirit was a valid New Testament doctrine. All doubt was gone in my heart and mind. I also concluded that God desired all of His children to have this experience.

Now back to the prayer meeting.

After 30 or so minutes of private, generalized prayer, I told the brothers present that I was ready to experience the Holy Spirit baptism. I collected my thoughts, took a deep breath and stood up from the altar and walked cautiously, yet expectantly, to the center of the room. Each step I took was measured. I was nervous, but determined. I was more than ready to encounter Him and His fullness. Little did I know that what followed in that church would change my life, my family and thousands of others, as well.

I will never forget the scene; it is forever etched into my mind. They all circled around me and began praying. They asked God to fill me with His Spirit. They prayed with such assurance as if knowing God would do what they asked. I never had seen such faith.

As they continued to pray, my heart was hungering for all of Him. I longed for everything He had for me, and I was

57

committed not to leave until His power came upon me just as it did in the book of Acts.

Nothing Happened, Except...

There I was, ready to receive, standing in front of four godly men. They gently walked toward me and after a short time of worshiping the Lord, each one laid his hands on me. I could hear them praying for me to be baptized with the Holy Spirit. It was powerful and sweet, **but "it" didn't happen**. Initially, on the first try, I didn't receive the baptism with the Holy Spirit.

> The more they prayed for me the tighter my throat became, it was as if something was constricting around my neck.

These seasoned ministers were not troubled by this. They knew I was a hard case due to my background. They were patient and continued to speak the Word of God over me, all the while, building my faith. They continually asked God to fill me. I was so hungry for God, but I was a little disappointed that it didn't happen immediately.

Then something shifted. The more they prayed for me the tighter my throat became, it was as if something was constricting around my neck. This had never happened before, and it was an awkward experience. I was having a hard time swallowing, but I knew God was doing something and I felt I was close to receiving the baptism with the Holy Spirit.

I interrupted and told them what was happening to my throat and neck. They calmly said, that is your prayer language trying to come forth and the enemy is trying to stop it. I believed it.

Renounce False Teaching

One of the pastors strolled slowly in front of me; he paused to analyze the situation. He weighed no more than one hundred forty pounds soaking wet; however, to me, in the Spirit realm, he was the Incredible Hulk. I could sense he had something to say. He did.

He looked into my eyes with compassion and assurance and authoritatively said, "Todd, you need to renounce all false doctrine and teaching you received over your lifetime regarding the baptism with the Holy Spirit."

I hadn't even thought about that, but it sounded reasonable. I nodded my head in agreement and closed my eyes. I took a slow, deep breath and, with brokenness, asked the Lord to forgive me for not believing His Word, and then, out loud, I renounced the false doctrine and teaching I had believed.

I further confessed that I wholeheartedly believed the baptism with the Holy Spirit is real and for me. The VERY MOMENT I repented and renounced the incorrect doctrine, my throat started to loosen and all my muscles relaxed.

At that moment, this skinny man of God softly placed his slender right index finger on my forehead and gave a gentle but charged command, **"Be filled with the Holy Spirit!"**

That is all he said; he didn't yell and shout at me or scream at the devil - he simply commanded me to be **"filled with the Holy Spirit."** And precisely at that moment, the Spirit of

God came upon me and I received the fullness of the Holy Spirit.

The Holy Spirit flooded my spirit. In all of my years, I had never encountered Him in such a way. I was overwhelmed and completely submerged in His love. He CAME UPON me and closely held me. I felt safe and full. His power penetrated every pore in my body.

Immediately, I was so overcome with God's presence that I fell to the floor. I literally couldn't stand under the weight of His glory; it was too much for my body to handle. Again, never before had anything like that happened to me. In fact, I used to mock and make light of such demonstrations.

To make things even more interesting, as soon as he touched me I began to speak in tongues. Yep, that's right. A Southern Baptist pastor speaking in tongues!

I have no doubt the enemy was trying to block this from happening by tightening my throat, but these men knew what I needed to do to unlock the precious ability to pray in the Spirit. This encounter has changed me forever.

On a side note, and one that I think is funny: Everything I called a sham, made fun of, ridiculed and preached against HAPPENED TO ME THAT MORNING!

All of it. Every bit of it.

It was amazing!

7

Paying
The Price

Have you ever had a gut feeling about something? I did.

Driving home, while still overwhelmed with what just happened, I suddenly had a sobering notion that some of my church members might have a "tiny" problem with my experience with the Holy Spirit.

I had pastored the church for over four years, and during that time, 3,000 people came to know Jesus. Many lives were changed. Everyone knew that our ministry had been tremendously effective and successful. The church was growing, adding families and building additional facilities to accommodate the new growth.

My logic? I thought, "Even if they didn't agree with me doctrinally, my members would respect my new walk with God and remain open and teachable."

Dynamite of God

My encounter with the Holy Spirit was so life-changing, I wanted to share it with the people I loved, my church family. I longed for them to experience the Holy Spirit the same way I did. So, within weeks, I began a preaching series entitled, *"The Dynamite of God."*

Things started well...

The first sermon I preached revealed how the Holy Spirit would help believers overcome the strongholds in their life. The presence of God was in the building. You could feel it. It was as if Heaven had come down and dwelled in our midst.

As I was preaching, people were totally captivated by the truths being shared and His hand seemed to be on every word. After the service, all of the comments I received were positive. I was very encouraged.

The following week the atmosphere was charged. The moment your foot stepped into the sanctuary you knew Jesus was in the room. Something fresh and beautiful was happening in my church. My heart rejoiced in their appetite to know Him more.

In my sermon I ministered on how the Holy Spirit would help us love Jesus more. Once again, the message was received well and the comments were affirming. Everybody seemed to be on board.

As momentum continued to build, the third week, the Lord directed me to preach about Peter's life before his encounter with the Holy Spirit on the day of Pentecost and to contrast that with his life after his encounter with the Spirit of God.

Inside my picturesque church building with its stained glass and padded pews, the atmosphere was electric. God was doing a deep work in all of our hearts and we all knew it. Once again, as I preached, people were on the edge of their seats, hanging on every word. They were thirsty for God. As I taught, I methodically made the case regarding the irrefutable difference the Holy Spirit made in Peter's life.

When it came time to give the altar call, I distinctly remember asking the congregation if they wanted to have the same encounter with the Holy Spirit that Peter had. People all over the congregation said, "Yes! Yes! Yes!"

Their affirmative response surprised me. I remember standing behind the pulpit and saying to myself, "Now what? How do I make this happen? What do I do?"

Here is something funny. I had only been baptized with the Holy Spirit a few weeks. I was so new in my walk with the Spirit, I didn't know how to lead others into having an encounter with the Holy Spirit. I couldn't let them know I didn't know what to do, so I had to think of something quick.

Then it hit me: stall, buy some time. I stepped forward to the edge of the stage and confidently said, as if it was the plan all along, "If you want to have the same experience Peter had, come back next Sunday and I will pray for you."

Embarrassingly, I needed the extra week to find out how to make it happen for them.

Once again, following the service dozens of people came to me and enthusiastically said they needed and wanted that kind of power. The hunger was unprecedented. Needless to say, momentum, excitement and anticipation were building in my Baptist Church.

So far, so good.

"This is easier than I anticipated. No major problems; everybody seems to be moving forward right on schedule," I thought.

I knew the upcoming Sunday was going to be special. During the week I received phone calls and had private meetings to discuss my experience. People were inquisitive and wanted to know more. They were so hungry and desperate for all God had for them. I felt that I was living in the book of Acts.

> I couldn't believe my eyes as I watched **over 70 Southern Baptists** come to the altar desperately wanting to be baptized with the Holy Spirit.

The following Sunday worship service was once again charged, and the sanctuary was filled to capacity.

It was the fourth week of my sermon series. At the conclusion of my message, I will never forget what happened! I encouraged those present who wanted to encounter the power of God to stay after the service for prayer. I dismissed the congregation and anxiously waited to see if anyone would remain behind. I couldn't believe my eyes as I watched **over 70 Southern Baptists** come to the altar desperately wanting to be baptized with the Holy Spirit.

64

My heart was filled with joy! To be honest, I was also shocked as I thought to myself, "Oh, no! How are we going to pray for all these people?"

It was a glorious morning as people of all ages were baptized with the Holy Spirit. As you can imagine, word began to spread throughout the community that something unusual was happening at that country Baptist Church.

The Calm Before The Storm

As we celebrated, a storm was brewing among many at the church. A well orchestrated coalition of opposition was mounting. At first it was a subtle underground movement organized to quietly squelch what God was doing in our church.

However, before I knew it a large percentage of the church arrayed themselves in religious armor and readied themselves for war. For example, an extensive "phone ministry" was started, as concerned church members shared with one another their fears and frustrations. They felt like their Baptist heritage was being threatened and that I was going to turn our church into a charismatic, aisle-running, tongue-chattering, pew-jumping church.

Even though the opposition was growing in number as well as influence, it didn't keep us from pushing forward with the message of the fullness of God. Nor did it keep those who were truly hungry from entering into this blessed new walk with God.

Those of us who were newly baptized in the Spirit were on fire. Joy and an infusion of power filled our lives. However, as the days and weeks passed, the "resistance" increased and gained considerable strength. It was difficult for me to watch the church that I loved deeply become divided into two camps.

8

Shaking Under The Power Of God

████████████████████████████████

I love optimistic people; they never give up and are always looking for the positive in every situation. I am reminded of the story about the optimist who accidentally fell from the roof of the one-hundred story building. Someone down on the fiftieth floor heard him, as he fell past an open window, saying, "So Far So Good!"

I am an optimistic person and I enthusiastically thought that most of our people would embrace all the wonderful things God was doing. But, as we all know, things don't always go as planned; sometimes your train of plans derails.

I read somewhere: "Don't complain because roses have thorns, smile because thorns have roses." On more than one occasion, I was having a hard time finding the roses in our situation.

Keep in mind, I was pastoring a thriving Southern Baptist church and we were seeing people, after receiving prayer, fall on the floor, speak in tongues and shake under the power of God.

These things never happen in most Baptist churches. Understandably, these manifestations deeply troubled some. My people didn't understand what was happening, and certainly didn't know what to expect next. A lot of what was taking place was new to me, as well. Needless to say, over the next several months we had some extremely interesting deacon, staff and leadership meetings.

In the midst of the fog of war, Karen and I kept moving forward. We knew that what was happening in people's lives was real. Not once did we ever doubt the validity and necessity of the baptism with the Holy Spirit.

We loved each person in our church, and it broke our hearts that some didn't support us or approve of what we were doing. Some of their actions and comments to us about the manifestations we were seeing were troubling, to say the least.

I remember vividly one church leader saying to me that what was going on was not of God. Another person said that what was taking place was demonic. One commented that I was teaching false doctrine. Still another well meaning brother said, "If you're going in this direction, then I'm leaving the church." And he did.

Our days were like riding a roller coaster, with high points and deep drops, and with quick unexpected turns and twists. One moment we would be filled with thrills and be in absolute awe at what God was doing, but then a few minutes later we would close our eyes and hang on for dear life. Joy and fear were the norm, like wacky cousins showing up on a whim only to box with one another.

We were experiencing the greatest days of our young ministry and yet, we were discouraged because so many people that we loved didn't embrace what God was doing.

In a short, three-month period, over one hundred people left the church, which is the last thing you want when you are in the process of building a new one-thousand-seat sanctuary. Many of my leaders became extremely uneasy and distraught. But, praise God, even though people were walking out the back door, God was sending new people through the front door.

God blessed us and, in just four months, we witnessed more than one hundred lost people come to know Jesus as Savior. Plus, many mighty deliverances took place. We witnessed strongholds being broken off people's lives as they were gloriously being set free. The power of God was present, validating our message and direction. However, many of the members of the church didn't interpret the new growth as God's stamp of approval.

Personal Attacks

In the beginning, opposition mainly centered on doctrinal differences. However, over time it escalated into personal attacks. People began to question my integrity and often attacked my character. I spent hours wondering how God's people could be so cruel. Often times, Karen and I cried ourselves to sleep.

Though there are many examples I could give you, one particular attack stands out in my mind. It was mid-November and I was in Wichita, Kansas, preaching for a dear friend. While I was away one of my church members, whom I loved and often ministered to, placed a prayer request in the offering plate during the Sunday morning service. The request read, "Please pray that Todd doesn't return from Kansas. The day will come when we will get our church back."

I knew some people wanted me to leave the church, but this note indicated they wanted more than that; maybe they wanted me dead.

The following week when I returned to the office, they delivered the note to me. I read it, read it again, and read it once more, each time slower than before. I stared at it in disbelief. My heart was crushed and, to be honest, I was completely devastated. Every word from the note had a suffocating effect on me. It was like someone stuck a knife in my heart and twisted the blade.

I quickly realized things were at a new level of vitriol. I knew some people wanted me to leave the church, but this note indicated they wanted more than that; maybe they wanted me dead.

A particularly dramatic incident stands out in all the turmoil. On a Sunday morning, when I was preaching a message on the "Power of God," I could sense His guiding hand upon me. Three-quarters of the way through the message, a man stood up, made his way into the aisle and started walking toward the front. It startled me and most of the congregation.

I didn't know what he was going to do, so I just kept preaching. He kept walking until he collapsed on the altar and began to weep and cry out for God to touch him. We were all amazed!

Right there, even before the altar call was officially given, in the middle of the preaching, he was miraculously saved and delivered from a haunting drug addiction.

Mind you, during my tenure at the church, no one had ever come forward in the middle of my sermon to be saved. God's convicting presence was so intense the man could not wait. Jesus was in the house!

Some in the church, however, started circulating the rumor that I planted the man in our service in order to gain supporters. In other words, I had manipulated the whole event and the man coming forward was staged for my benefit. If that wasn't enough, it was even said that I paid the man to come to the altar.

Needless to say I was startled and hurt, but not sidetracked. We continued preaching the truth. We dug in. I heard it said, "A river cuts through rock, not because of its power, but because of its persistence."

We were motivated to introduce as many people as possible to the remarkable encounter with the Holy Spirit. I knew we were in the center of God's will and nothing could deter us. Not one time did I doubt our teachings or our motives. God's hand was upon me and my wife, and we knew it.

Day of Visitation

After my encounter with the Holy Spirit, we saw people saved by the dozens, but that is not all. For the first time we were experiencing miracles and healings.

For example, one of our precious ladies had been suffering from chronic migraine headaches. The doctors ordered an x-ray and her worst nightmare was realized: a tumor.

The Sunday School class she attended was notified of her diagnosis and decided to anoint her with oil and lay hands on her. They prayed the prayer of faith over her in obedience to James 5:14-15. Afterward, she said she felt the power of God come on her as they laid their hands on her head. She was instantly healed and the tumor dissolved by the power of God.

Imagine that! A group of Baptist believers practicing the Word and then seeing Jesus confirm the Word!

*"And they went out and preached everywhere, **the Lord working with them** and **confirming the word through the accompanying signs**."* (Mark 16:20)

The finger of God was at work in our church. Unfortunately, too many in the congregation were failing to recognize that it was God that was visiting us in power. They were being blinded by the enemy and, therefore, could not see the truth.

I felt like they were following in the same footsteps of the children of Israel. Throughout the New Testament we read how Jesus walked among the Jews in power as the Son of God, and how He performed miracle after miracle, yet His own children did not receive him. John 1:11 says, *"He came to His own, and His own did not receive Him."*

In Luke's Gospel, chapter 19, it is reported that Jesus stopped on a hillside and looked down over the city of Jerusalem. How long He paused and gazed at His beloved city is unknown. However, it was long enough for His emotions to surface. The Bible says, *"Jesus wept."*

Why did Jesus become so emotional? Why was He crying? The Bible is clear on this matter: He wept because His people did not recognize *"their day of visitation."* Jesus, God's only Son, walked among them and they received Him not. This broke the heart of Jesus.

I was convinced our church was being visited by God. I had never seen or experienced God in such a tangible way. Every day my heart was overflowing with joy and anticipation. However, the attitudes, reactions and comments of the people in our church shouted, "I am not interested!"

It was as if they were declaring, "If this is it, then I don't want it!"

9

The Departure

Even though God was doing marvelous things in our midst it became evident to Karen and me that we needed to move on. We both knew it was just a matter of time before we were going to receive the "left foot of fellowship." The number of those who wanted me gone was growing and their voice was getting louder.

I Knew Why They Came

I will never forget my last Wednesday night at the church. It was our monthly church conference, our business meeting. It is in these meetings that members of the church can vote to approve or disapprove of the church's decisions and direction. In most Baptist churches the people decide when a pastor should come and when a pastor should leave. On this particular July night, the church was to have such a vote. I knew the evening would be difficult for me and my family. However, we were holding onto the hand that held onto us.

A dear friend drove me to the church that night; it was a short five minute drive, but it felt like an eternity. Not much was said, if anything. I stared out the window and as mailboxes and trees whisked by, a million thoughts raced through my mind.

As we made the slow turn around the bend in the road, I could see a sea of cars in the parking lot. This wasn't typical for a Wednesday night. My heart rate increased dramatically - I could feel each thump as my heart pounded in my chest. They came by the carload and I knew why they came; they came to take back their church. In fact, a good number of people present had not darkened those church doors for years. However, on this night they were there to cast their vote to decide the direction of the church. I knew in just a matter of a few minutes my life would be forever altered. At no time in my life did I feel so alone, and yet at the same time, so at peace.

As I walked through the doors that I had walked through hundreds of times, I made my way to the front row and I sat down. As I looked around, my mind was reminiscing about all the good things that happened at that country church. The thousands that were saved, the families that were restored, the young people who decided to follow Jesus into full-time ministry. The funerals, the baptisms, the weddings, the baby dedications - it all came flashing before my eyes. I thought about the countless Saturday-night prayer meetings where we would gather together to seek the face of God, oftentimes praying well into the morning. We would weep and plead with the Lord for souls. I was filled with heavenly emotion, but I knew in my heart my time had come to an end. I was entering that building for the last time.

Prior to the business meeting the Lord spoke to my heart about establishing a new church in Gainesville, Georgia, where I could preach the whole counsel of God without resistance. My wife and I submitted to God's desire. So that night, before the church had a chance to dismiss me, I stepped to the platform and resigned my position as senior pastor and announced a new church would be founded the following Sunday. Since that night, God has taken me and my family on an unimaginable journey.

Many have asked, "Would you do it over again?" Without hesitation I say, "Absolutely! You bet I would." I would willingly go through the same things - the hurt, rejection, betrayal, ridicule and adversity. The reason I can say that is because I know the baptism with the Holy Spirit is real. I know it's the truth. I would die for it if need be.

I will not turn back! I can't turn back! My eyes have seen too much and my ears have heard too much.

78

Section Two

"Overcoming The Obstacles"

10

An 18-Wheeler Tells The Truth

A friend of mine, Craig Toney, was in his car and an 18 wheeler passed him on the freeway. On the rear slide up door of this tractor trailer was an advertisement for a particular vacuum cleaner. The caption caught his eye, it read, ***"Presentation without DEMONSTRATION is just conversation."***

Interesting, huh? What's the message?

You need an in-person demonstration. In other words, DO NOT BUY a vacuum cleaner unless you see with your own eyes what it can actually do.

We all know vacuum cleaner salespersons can bloviate at times over the wonderful features and capabilities of their machine. They can and will brag that their product, due to advanced engineering, has unequaled power to remove dirt, grime, hair and allergens from the carpet.

However, without an in-home demonstration, it leaves one to wonder if what the salesperson is saying is valid.

So this is good advice: MAKE THEM DEMONSTRATE before you buy.

He Demonstrated!

Immediately after He turned the water into wine, the ministry and popularity of Jesus erupted. Word quickly spread, and soon people saw and heard that there was a man who had extraordinary power to heal the sick, cure diseases, cleanse the lepers, cast out demons and even raise the dead. The masses traveled for days and traversed great obstacles just to see Him, and at times upwards of 20,000 people came to behold Him. They knew just a simple touch of His hand would mean they would never be the same.

Jesus brazenly used signs and wonders to **demonstrate** His benevolent nature and to reveal the goodness of the Father. While not everyone believed on Him because of the miracles, many did. The scriptures say,

*"Now when He was in Jerusalem at the Passover, during the feast, **many believed in His name when they saw the signs which He did.**"* (John 2:23)

Unbelievers all over the world are somewhat familiar with Jesus and the gospel story. Their perspective is diverse and not always positive. Tragically, for many, Jesus and the life He lived are nothing more than a small, insignificant piece of history, or worse yet, a noteworthy fairy tale. Along the same lines, some say that Jesus was a good man who did admirable things, while others say He was a prophet or teacher, but not much more.

The following question begs to be asked:

What can we do to help convince the ever-growing segment of society that are unbelieving, cynical and averse toward Christ, that the Jesus story is more than a blip on the radar of history? What can be done that will cause skeptics to take another honest look at Christ?

ANSWER:

We can provide a consistent portrayal of God's love that is coupled with a visible, physical demonstration of God's power.

People need to see His power, not just hear about it.

It Started Strong, But...

Jesus birthed the church with a fiery explosion. It came at the speed of a camera flash. The might of heaven invaded an inconspicuous room that was a temporary gathering place for one hundred twenty desperate people. The event was so violent, fierce and uncontrollable that those in the streets scurried to investigate what had happened.

> I wonder when people outside our church buildings will hear the sound of heaven inside and rush in to find out what is going on?

I wonder when people outside our church buildings will hear the sound of heaven inside and rush in to find out what is going on?

Believe it or not there is a large segment within the body of Christ that believes miracles, signs and wonders are no longer necessary, nor available in the 21st century. They are called cessationists. In short, they believe the age of miracles and the supernatural ceased at the death of the last apostle.

If one holds this view, then they have to intellectually deal with the following question: "Why would Jesus ever strip or take away the power and the ability of His children to perform signs and wonders that would only help convince the world of His goodness and ability to save?"

In the following two verses, Jesus candidly revealed His intent for the Church.

*"Most assuredly, I say to you, he who believes in Me, **the works that I do he will do also;** and greater works than these he will do, because I go to My Father."* (John 14:12)

*"Behold, I send the Promise of My Father upon you; but tarry in the city of Jerusalem until you are **endued with power** from on high."* (Luke 24:49)

His instruction and promise of power to fulfill His mission hasn't changed.

Take a look at the verses again. Do you see an **"expiration date"** anywhere? Is there a **time limit** on His power? What about something that says, **"Best if used by...."**? Is there **small prin**t somewhere on the page, perhaps in the margin, that says, **"Valid until the last apostle dies"**?

I looked and can't seem to find any of those statements anywhere! Yet, our pulpits and seminaries are filled with this inexcusable nonsense. This is what I was taught in seminary. No wonder I never saw any miracles!

I can envision Jesus sitting on a rock addressing His disciples who are gathered around. He begins to outline the upcoming days. "Ok," he says, "You guys will have power to cast out devils, lay hands on the sick, raise the dead and cure diseases. But after the last one of you dies all of that stuff will come to an end."

> Those early disciples simply believed the words of Jesus and acted on what He said.

Do you see the intellectual lunacy in this?

No place in the Bible does it say or even imply that the Church cannot operate and function like the believers did in the book of Acts. Those early disciples simply believed the words of Jesus and acted on what He said. He told them,

*"Go into all the world and preach the gospel to every creature...And **these signs will follow those who believe**; In My name **they will cast out demons**; **they will speak with new tongues**; they will take up serpents; and if they drink anything deadly, it will by no means hurt them; **they will lay hands on the sick, and they will recover.**"* (Mark 16:15, 17-18)

Disturbingly, whole doctrines have been built around the notion that the gifts of the Spirit are no longer available in the Church. Plus, they claim that the ability to perform miracles by the Spirit of God is no longer available, nor necessary.

This erroneous ideology and understanding of scripture has spewed forth from our pulpits and seminaries for several decades in America, if not the world, and it has stripped the Church of any expectation to be able to experience and walk in the supernatural. Overwhelmingly, by choice, the brand of Christianity that is on display in most churches is "conversation" without demonstration. We are comfortable with conversation.

It's simple. Thoughtful. Cerebral. Analytical. Subjective. Intellectual. And, may I add, it is usually uneventful and borderline boring. There is little or no wonderment and fascination; "conversation" is typically theoretical with nothing visible. Furthermore, it doesn't require anything from us other more than to be good listeners with an occasional nod of the head. No action is expected; therefore, we are never disappointed.

Again, vast amounts of people like to go to conversation-only-oriented churches. These churches are easy to attend. The sermons are usually helpful, the songs are inspiring, and the "church experience" is generally uplifting and edifying. You generally have a good time and are comforted at every level.

However, I have discovered and witnessed firsthand that **when people who attend conversation-only churches find themselves in a crisis demanding more than theory, explanation of terms and well-packaged belief systems, they will seek out the DEMONSTRATORS**. They come looking for people and churches that believe for more and expect more, people who actively demonstrate God's power.

Today, God is raising up a segment within His Church that refuse to be conversation-only Christians. They desire to demonstrate His will and power.

Paul said it this way:

*"And my speech and my preaching were not with persuasive words of human wisdom, but in **DEMONSTRATION** of the Spirit and of power, that your faith should not be in the wisdom of men but in the **power of God**."* (1 Corinthians 2:4, 5)

The Holy Spirit was given to the Church in order to manifest God's goodness and power to a lost world. God never intended for the Church to lose the power from which it started.

This is the era of demonstration.

The Church must demonstrate. In order for that to happen, we all need an encounter with the Holy Spirit.

11

"We Don't Believe That!"

Before my encounter with the Holy Spirit I had to overcome a plethora of obstacles. Like me, you may have questions that need to be answered and scriptures that need to be explained. In order for you to accurately prepare yourself for the baptism with the Holy Spirit, you must address those mental, spiritual and denominational barriers.

While I was in the process of teaching my Baptist church about the baptism with the Holy Spirit, I often heard, "But Todd, we are Baptists and we don't believe that way." Another would say, "Our denomination doesn't teach this." Then someone else might remark, "This teaching is divisive and, therefore, can't be from the Lord." One of my favorites was, "I'm confused, and the Bible says, 'God is not the author of confusion,' so this can't be God's will."

Comments like these were recurring. I couldn't be too judgmental because I used to say the same things. But, as I prayed and studied, I realized that such thinking was misguided, ill-informed and unfortunate. It played directly into the hands of the enemy.

One afternoon, I received a phone call from a church member that was no longer attending our services due to my experience and teaching regarding the Holy Spirit. After the courteous generalities, I asked him what was on his mind. Well, that opened the door for a disturbing comment that shook me to the core. I'll never forget what he said. "There is nothing scripturally wrong with your teaching on the baptism with the Holy Spirit," he emphatically told me. Then he added that he was raised Southern Baptist and he didn't believe this experience should be taught in a Baptist church. He concluded by saying that he chose **not to believe and practice that portion of the Bible!**

I was shocked! I could not believe what I heard. I responded by saying, "Brother, one day you are going to stand before God and He is going to ask you about your obedience to His Word. What do you suppose God is going to say to you when you tell him you refused to practice, believe and obey a portion of His Word because you were Baptist?" I told him God was not going to be pleased with his position. He understood and saw my point and, needless to say, the conversation ended shortly thereafter.

Just think about it. Can you imagine standing before God and explaining to Him why you did not obey a part of His Word because of the church you attended?

"Well, God, you see I was a _____ and I didn't believe in the baptism with the Holy Spirit."

"God, we didn't allow the spiritual gifts to operate because we were concerned with offending someone."

Or one might say this:

"We didn't practice that part because we were afraid of someone speaking in tongues."

Honestly, how do you think God will respond to such rationale?

We must remember that we are Christians before we are Methodists, Pentecostals, Baptists or Presbyterians. His Word must take precedence over our denominational teachings and creeds. Our loyalty and adherence is to Him and His Word, not to our church handbook or church constitution. God's Word is our sole authority and nothing should supersede or replace it.

Before we continue, I must make several comments.

First, contrary to some thinking, Jesus was not, and is not, a Baptist, a Methodist or a Pentecostal.

Second, the Word of God was not written so we could pick and choose what we want to believe or don't want to believe. The sixty-six books of the Bible reveal the whole heart and counsel of God. Every word of the Bible is for our benefit. It is His master plan for our lives. If we choose to ignore a particular section, chapter or verse because we belong to a certain group or are uncomfortable with its application, then we are sinning against Him and falling short of His perfect plan for our lives.

Sadly, as I have observed firsthand, some people are more devoted to their denomination than to the Word of God. This is wrong.

God desires for you to walk in obedience to His Word, His whole Word, the complete Word.

12

Speaking In Tongues

A kindergarten teacher was walking around observing her classroom of children while they drew pictures. As she got to one girl working diligently, she asked what the drawing was.

The girl replied, "I'm drawing God." The teacher paused and said, "But no one knows what God looks like." Without looking up from her drawing, the girl responded, "They will in a minute."

I believe that in the next few minutes you will have a better understanding of the controversial subject of "speaking in tongues." I want to "draw" for you the real intent and purpose of this wonderful gift.

To be honest, this was one of the largest obstacles I had to overcome in order to receive the baptism with the Holy Spirit.

My mind was inundated with inaccurate information; therefore, my reference points for this blessed manifestation were limited, or better yet, tainted.

Generally, I looked down upon those who spoke in tongues and thought it was simply weirdo babbling. Throughout the years, I was often warned by teachers and preachers I respected about the rampant misuse and evils of speaking in tongues, and as a result, I was extremely skeptical regarding it, even close-minded. In fact, I wanted nothing to do with it.

I now understand the immense value of tongues and its significance to the body of Christ. You have to remember, as a Baptist preacher I taught against tongues. Boy, was I operating in ignorance!

Like me, most believers today are scared to death of tongues. Why? No one has accurately taught them what the Bible says about the subject.

I want to teach you.

Least of The Gifts? Not So!

Over the years, and on multiple occasions, I've heard people say, "The Bible teaches that tongues is the least of the gifts." I believed that; therefore, I concluded that it wasn't that important.

The problem with that belief is that it is not scriptural. I challenge anyone to find that statement in the Bible. It isn't there. There's not even a hint that speaking in tongues is the least gift.

I know some people base that statement on the premise that the gift of "tongues" is mentioned last in the spiritual gift list of 1 Corinthians 12:10. However, if that is the basis for judging significance and importance, then what about what Paul says about the fruit of the spirit in Galatians 5:22-23?

*"But the fruit of the Spirit is love, joy, peace, longsuffering, kindness, goodness, faithfulness, gentleness, **self-control**...."*

Or, when Jesus referred to Peter, James and John, did that mean John was the least of them? We must not forget that it was the beloved disciple, John, who held a special place in Jesus' heart.

Just because something is mentioned last in a list doesn't mean it is last in purpose or priority. It should be obvious that in any list, something has to appear last, without any regard to its value relative to the rest of the list. Therefore, you can't develop a doctrinal position based upon placement in a list.

There Are Different Types of Tongues

Believe it or not, there is more than one type of tongue mentioned in the Bible. Yep, that is correct. Paul in his teaching to the church clarified the different types of tongues.

First, there is what many leaders call a **"public tongue."** This is a spiritual gift given to individual members within the body of Christ; it is mentioned in 1 Corinthians 12:10, and is called a public tongue because it's to be exercised openly during the gathering of believers and nonbelievers.

Acts 2 and 1 Corinthians 14 shed valuable insight on the usage of this gift publicly during worship.

Here are several factors to consider:

When one takes a close look at Acts 2 you can see the Lord using tongues as an **evangelistic tool**.

Acts 2:4-14a: *"And they were all filled with the Holy Spirit and began to speak with other tongues, as the Spirit gave them utterance. And there were dwelling in Jerusalem Jews, devout men, from every nation under heaven. And when this sound occurred, the multitude came together, and were confused, because everyone heard them speak in his own language. Then they were all amazed and marveled, saying to one another, 'Look, are not all these who speak Galileans? And how is it that we hear, each in our own language in which we were born? Parthians and Medes and Elamites, those dwelling in Mesopotamia, Judea and Cappadocia, Pontus and Asia, Phrygia and Pamphylia, Egypt and the parts of Libya adjoining Cyrene, visitors from Rome, both Jews and proselytes, Cretans and Arabs—we hear them speaking in our own tongues the wonderful works of God.' So they were all amazed and perplexed, saying to one another, 'Whatever could this mean?' Others mocking said, 'They are full of new wine.' But Peter, standing up with the eleven, raised his voice and said to them…."*

What is truly astounding is that verses 7 and 8 reveal that onlookers and outsiders were ***amazed*** and ***marveled*** at what they saw and heard. Verse 11 states the bystanders heard these early disciples ***"speak the wonderful works of God."***

One can accurately conclude this wondrous manifestation of God's power opened the door for Peter to preach the wonderful news of Jesus to the curious crowd. As a result 3,000 people believed and were saved. (Acts 2:41)

We should not undervalue the public use of tongues in our worship services. If utilized correctly, it will be a tool God uses to open up hearts and minds to the gospel.

Paul Corrected the Church

Shortly after the Church was established in Corinth, some within the body evidently misused and/or misunderstood tongues. Paul addressed their concerns in 1 Corinthians 12-14.

A. He outlined for all believers the proper usage for tongues. Paul stated, when a public tongue is given, there must be an interpreter.

1 Corinthians 14:27,28: *"If anyone speaks in a tongue, let there be two or at the most three, each in turn, and let one interpret. But if there is no interpreter, let him keep silent in church, and let him speak to himself and to God."*

Let me add, in the case that no one interprets a public tongue, it doesn't mean the person giving the tongue was out of order or missed God's leading. Perhaps, the person who was supposed to deliver the interpretation failed to step out in faith and give it. They may have been afraid and, therefore, remained silent.

All parties involved must be encouraged to obey the Spirit and yield to His promptings.

B. Paul warned against everyone speaking in tongues at the same time in a public gathering. The unbeliever and even the uninformed will think those speaking in tongues have lost their minds.

> All appeared normal and just when I was getting comfortable, "it" happened.

1 Corinthians 14:23: *"Therefore if the whole church comes together in one place, and all speak with tongues, and there come in those who are uninformed or unbelievers, will they not say that you are out of your mind?"*

I was 15 years old and a relatively new Christian when I first walked through the doors of a Pentecostal church. I had heard about such places, so I was nervous and excited at the same time. The atmosphere was electric, the room was packed, everyone seemed to want to be there, the music was upbeat and the crowd was singing and clapping. Surprisingly, I was thoroughly enjoying all elements of the service. All appeared normal and just when I was getting comfortable, "it" happened.

Yep, you guessed it; as if on cue, everyone around me began speaking in tongues. This was my first real exposure to tongues and I was trying really hard not to stare at people but I couldn't help it. My eyes got as big as basketballs. It more than startled me, it scared me.

One moment they were completely normal and then "bam" they got weird on me. I felt so out of place, and desperately wanted to leave. Remember, I was brought up Baptist, and not one time had I ever heard or seen this sort of thing. Truthfully, I thought the people were crazy as if they were under some type of a spell. Over time, it was experiences like this that helped develop my negative view of speaking in tongues.

The second type of tongues mentioned in the Bible is the **"private tongue,"** which is often referred to as "praying in the Spirit," the "devotional tongue" or "spirit language."

I will never forget the moment I discovered that the Apostle Paul

> Truthfully, I had to read it several times to make sure I wasn't reading something that wasn't there.

mentioned this type of tongue. When I read this text it literally exploded in my spirit - it was like a fireworks display in my head and heart. I remember saying to myself, "There it is...there it is! Right there in scripture, there it is...." Truthfully, I had to read it several times to make sure I wasn't reading something that wasn't there. Not one time in my life had I ever seen this scripture - well, I know I had, but my denominational glasses prevented me from really seeing what it was actually saying.

1 Corinthians 14:
"For if I PRAY IN A TONGUE my spirit prays, but my understanding is unfruitful. What is the conclusion then? I WILL PRAY WITH THE SPIRIT, and I will also pray with the understanding...."

The Apostle Paul makes a significant connection between prayer and tongues. This is completely different from the "public tongue" that he refers to in the same chapter. The "public tongue" needs an interpreter, the "private tongue" does not, as it is to be used in a time of private prayer, thanksgiving and intercession.

This is where people have the most difficulty. They don't see the difference between the "public" tongue and the "private" tongue. They inappropriately lump them together. The Scriptures teach us that these two types of tongues are unique and have a defined role for the believer and the Church. To receive the full benefit of each tongue we must understand their purpose.

Many people have asked the following questions: "Why do we need to pray in tongues?" and/or, "Is it really that important?"

Purpose of Praying In Tongues
(Praying in the Spirit)

1. Praying in tongues allows you to speak/pray **"divine mysteries"** unto the Lord.

"For he who speaks in a tongue does not speak to men but to God, for no one understands him; however, <u>in the spirit</u> he SPEAKS MYSTERIES." (1 Corinthians 14:2)

I think the Contemporary English Version says it best:

*"If you speak languages that others don't know, God will understand what you are saying, though no one else will know what you mean. **You will be talking about mysteries that only the Spirit understands.**"* (1 Corinthians 14:2)

The Good News Translation of the same verse above says, when we speak in tongues we are **"speaking secret truths by the Spirit."** Wow! Don't miss the seriousness and depth of this. You and I have the supernatural ability to pray divine secrets unto the Lord. Literally, no one understands what I am praying, not even the devil. Here is the great news: God

100

gives this ability to "pray in tongues" to every believer that experiences the baptism with the Holy Spirit.

It gets better...

2. You "edify" or "build yourself up."

1 Corinthians 14:4 says, *"He who speaks in a tongue edifies himself."* In other words, we encourage and enlarge ourselves in the Lord. J.B. Phillips, says, "He who speaks in an unknown tongue builds himself up." I don't know about you, but I need to be built up and encouraged in my spirit each and every day.

The Amplified Bible translates verse 4 this way: *"He who speaks in a [strange] tongue...**improves himself.**"* This is amazing, absolutely wonderful! No wonder the devil wants to keep the body of Christ away from this blessed expression!

Again, this is available to all of us, regardless of our denominational background. Every child of God needs to see the value of praying in tongues. Praying in tongues helps you. It is to your advantage and benefit.

Jude adds his thoughts on praying in tongues.

*"But you, beloved, **BUILDING YOURSELVES UP** on your most holy faith, **PRAYING IN THE HOLY SPIRIT**...."* Jude 20

This passage encourages us to pray in the Spirit, and in doing so it "builds us up." It adds depth, structure and strength to our lives. It increases our stamina and helps us in building our faith. One of my friends said that when he prays in the Spirit, it is like his battery gets recharged.

I don't know about you, but there are times I get discouraged and feel flat in my faith. The enemy too often succeeds in knocking the wind out of me. However, when I pray in tongues I immediately feel better in my spirit. It is as if I catch my breath again.

The more you and I pray in tongues the stronger in the spirit we become.

When I was growing up I played with a toy airplane. It was an engineering wonder. You had a propeller connected to a rubber band. In order for the plane to fly, you had to twist the propeller, which would tighten the rubber band. When you couldn't tighten it anymore you knew the plane was ready to fly. At the precise moment, you would let the plane go and it would soar through the air like a rocket. There are times when I am praying in tongues that I literally feel my spirit getting *wound up* for the Lord. I am being encouraged and built-up in Him. The more you and I pray in tongues, the stronger in the spirit we become.

3. I am able to pray for all the saints.

*"**PRAYING ALWAYS** with all **PRAYER** and supplication **IN THE SPIRIT**, being watchful to this end with all perseverance and supplication for **ALL THE SAINTS**."* (Ephesians 6:18)

Paul gives the command for us to pray for all the saints. To do that effectively is impossible for us in the natural. However, when we pray in tongues, it is possible. Here is the key: The Holy Spirit knows all things; therefore, He knows who needs prayer and when they need it.

John 16:13 tells us it is *"the Holy Spirit who will guide us into all truth."* Even though you don't know what or who you

102

should pray for, the Holy Spirit does. And, according to scripture, the Spirit of God will make intercession through you.

Have you ever been suddenly awakened in the middle of the night for no apparent reason? Don't treat this lightly. God is waking you up because He needs you to pray. Someone may be in trouble, perhaps a missionary in a third-world country, or even a member of your family may need divine intervention. God is getting you up to pray. He responds to the prayers of His children. At 3:00 AM, I may not know what to pray or who to pray for, so I immediately start praying in tongues. This frequently happens to me.

You should pray until you feel a release, or a level of peace comes to you. When the peace of God comes, it affirms that the "thing" or "issue" you were in prayer for has been resolved. Think about it, God is awakening you for a reason and your timely prayers could literally cause a divine intervention and perhaps save a person's life.

We don't know everything that we should pray for, but the Spirit knows all things. Praying in tongues allows us to pray what the Spirit of God needs us to pray.

4. My spirit prays.

*"For if I pray in a tongue, **my spirit prays**, but my understanding is unfruitful."* (1 Corinthians 14:14)

The Bible teaches us that God is Spirit. (John 4:24) He is a Spirit being. Furthermore, the Bible reveals that we, too, are spirit beings, only, housed in a body, our flesh.

According to Paul, when you and I pray in tongues, it is our spirit that prays. Whatever you do, don't miss that revelation. Praying in the spirit does not come from your logical mind; it comes from your spirit. It is at this very point that many fall short in understanding how praying in tongues actually works.

Again, when you pray in tongues, your spirit prays. You intentionally connect your spirit with your tongue. In other words, the prayers are coming directly from your spirit and not your head. When your spirit connects with your tongue, you give voice to your spirit.

Praying in tongues is one of the most spiritual things you will ever do. Naturally, your tongue and brain work in unison. Everything you say, your brain thinks about it first and then you give voice to it with your tongue. Your tongue is connected to your brain. Again, when you pray in tongues, your tongue is no longer connected to your natural brain, but connects with your spirit, which is divinely connected with the Spirit of God.

When I only pray from my head, my understanding is limited to my personal knowledge, that is, what I know and have experienced. However, when I pray from my spirit, in tongues, the possibilities are limitless. Why? My spirit is eternal and it is in communion with the Spirit of God who knows all things. This is why Paul said, *"I will pray in the spirit...."* (1 Corinthians 14:15)

Remember what happened on the day of Pentecost in Acts 2? Verse 4 says, *"And they were all filled with the Holy Spirit and began to speak with tongues, as **the Spirit gave them utterance."*** This doesn't mean the Spirit took over their vocal cords and forced them to speak. The Spirit "gave" them or "delivered" to them what to say, and out loud they boldly said what the Spirit gave them. Their minds didn't understand it because it bypassed their heads and came directly from their spirit.

One of the greatest joys about praying in tongues is knowing the Holy Spirit is giving you the utterance. In other words, the Spirit of God is telling your spirit what to pray. Therefore, you pray the **PERFECT will of God EVERY TIME!**

Romans 8:26 further highlights the benefit of praying in the spirit:

*"Likewise **the Spirit also helps in our weaknesses.** For we **do not know what we should pray for** as we ought, but the Spirit Himself makes intercession for us with groanings which cannot be uttered."* (Romans 8:26)

Shortly after being baptized with the Holy Spirit, I experienced, firsthand, the power and benefit of praying in tongues. It was a bitterly cold day in January and all hell was breaking loose in my church. On every side, the devil was wreaking havoc. It seemed every week another family was leaving the church, my heart was broken. Confidence in my leadership was slipping and my staff was confused and divided. Every day was a mixture of extraordinary highs and unbelievable lows. In my soul I was distraught and painfully discouraged.

I was alone in my office, and deep down on the inside I felt the need to pray. Being so new in my spirit walk, I didn't understand everything about praying in tongues. I practiced it but didn't understand the full impact it could have on people and situations. On this particular day my perspective dramatically changed.

As I sat in my office, I yielded to the Spirit and began to pray in tongues. The Holy Spirit swelled up on the inside of me and prayed through me for two uninterrupted hours. In my entire life, never had I prayed for two hours straight!

Have you ever witnessed a mouse running on a spinning wheel? It seems to be cruel as he desperately tries to keep up with the momentum created by the wheel. He runs and runs and runs. Well, that was me praying in the spirit. I couldn't keep up with what the Spirit of God wanted me to pray. At times I had to pause in order to catch my breath. It took everything I had in order to stay in step with Him, and pray all that He wanted me to pray. To top it all off, I didn't understand a single word I was saying, but I knew it was God. It was glorious and I was confident I had His full attention, and that I was praying the perfect will of God. I finished praying in tongues when the urgency lifted, and a sweet heavenly peace swept over me.

During that intense time of intercession, I must have prayed for souls to be saved and that our church would experience new growth and a spiritual breakthrough. The following four months over one hundred people gave their lives to Jesus, dozens of people were baptized with the Holy Spirit and new families were added to our congregation. I believe they came in direct response to that time of deep intercession.

Praying in tongues is one of the greatest gifts God has given to His children.

Receive, release and enjoy!

13

Can I Pray In Tongues?

This is a great question. People want to know if praying in tongues is for everyone or if it's reserved for a select few.

One day I decided to ask a prominent Pentecostal pastor what he thought. His answer was clever. He said, "Todd, when you buy a pair of shoes from the store the tongues come with it." He added, "When you get baptized with the Holy Spirit tongues come with the experience. They may not manifest at that moment, but the ability to pray in tongues is still there."

I am convinced every spirit-filled child of God has the ability to pray in tongues and should do so daily. It is truly God's best for your life and is one-hundred percent Biblical. Far too many believers think it is not for them, or that God doesn't want them to experience it. However, the Word says something different.

*"I wish you **ALL** spoke with tongues."* (1 Corinthians 14:5a)

Did you get what Paul just said? It's an actual Bible verse!

*"I wish **YOU ALL** spokes with tongues."*

Guess what? You are included in this verse. You are a part of the "YOU ALL." He didn't leave you out or overlook you; this covers you, me, all of us!

*"And they were **all** filled with the Holy Spirit and **began to speak with other tongues**, as the Spirit gave them utterance."* (Acts 2:4)

Whatever you do, don't miss the next thought. You have to catch it.

Do me a favor, before you read it, clear your mind and take a deep breath, because you will need it.

Are you ready?

Every one of Jesus' disciples that walked with Him and followed His earthly ministry was baptized with the Holy Spirit and spoke in tongues. **All of them encountered the Holy Spirit and spoke in tongues.**

There is more; even His own mother was baptized with the Holy Spirit and spoke in tongues. I am sure you would agree with me that if His disciples needed this encounter, so do you and I. Surely, you recall that they were among one hundred twenty disciples in an upper room when *"they were* all filled with the Holy Spirit, and began to speak with other tongues, as the Spirit gave them utterance." (Acts 2:4)

Did the Apostle Paul speak in tongues?

"...that you might receive your sight and be filled with the Holy Spirit." (Acts 9:17)

According to this passage there is no direct evidence that Paul spoke with other tongues, however, we know according to 1 Corinthians 14 that he prayed in tongues regularly and encouraged others to do so as well.

"I thank God **I speak in tongues** more than all of you...." (1 Corinthians 14:18)

We can safely assume that the beloved Apostle Paul received his prayer language the same time he was filled with the Spirit. He unapologetically proclaimed his delight in praying in tongues.

The Biblical precedent continues.

"While Peter was still speaking these words, the Holy Spirit fell upon all those who heard the word...**For they heard them speak with tongues** and magnify God." (Acts10:44, 46)

"When they heard this, they were baptized in the name of the Lord Jesus. And when Paul laid his hands on them, the Holy Spirit came upon them, and **they spoke with tongues and prophesied.**" (Acts 19:5, 6)

Whatever you do, please do not allow the devil, a good friend, a fellow church member, your denominational affiliation, even your pastor or your doubts to rob you of this blessed privilege. This experience is for you; it is God-given, God-powered, and God-honoring. In fact, Paul said,

"...do not forbid to speak in tongues." (1 Corinthians 14:39)

Anyone who tells you that you can't or shouldn't speak and pray in tongues is not congruent with the Word of God. Don't allow yourself to be cheated out of enjoying and engaging in all that the Father has for you.

It is important to note that speaking in tongues is not something the Holy Spirit all of a sudden does to you, but it's a way He flows and operates through you. He will not override your will, grab your tongue and force you to speak in tongues. God willingly cooperates with your spirit.

One of the most common concerns I hear from people is that they have a fear of "speaking in tongues" in their own strength, in other words, making "it" happen. They want the experience to be pure, genuine, authentic, and something God does to and for them. I understand their concern and God knows their heart and sees their hunger. I want your faith to rise, so read this text slowly,

"For everyone who asks receives, and he who seeks finds, and to him who knocks it will be opened. 11 If a son asks for bread from any father among you, will he give him a stone? Or if he asks for a fish, will he give him a serpent instead of a fish? 12 Or if he asks for an egg, will he offer him a scorpion? 13 If you then, being evil, know how to give good gifts to your children, how much more will your heavenly Father give the Holy Spirit to those who ask Him!" (Luke 11:10-13)

The key to receiving your prayer language is faith. God isn't going to just make this happen. You have to speak by faith. It is something God wants to do through you and it requires your cooperation. At first, it might seem like human effort, but you must start to speak from your spirit.

I know it may be difficult to lay aside your insecurities and concerns, but I encourage you to start speaking from your spirit. Give voice to your spirit. You may ask, what does that mean? As I said in the previous chapter, just as my tongue is connected to my brain and I verbalize what my brain thinks, now connect your tongue to your spirit man and verbalize what your spirit is saying.

Let me illustrate it this way. The process of praying in the spirit is like putting a key into the ignition of a car.

> ...now connect your tongue to your spirit man and verbalize what your spirit is saying.

The car will not start by itself. You must turn the key in the ignition. Praying in tongues will not start all by itself. You turn the key by starting to speak in faith, not in your known language, but by giving voice to the utterances coming forth from your spirit. Don't worry about what it sounds like or if it makes sense. It is a new language coming forth from your spirit that you will not understand.

Also, the more you pray in tongues, the more proficient you will become. The more you exercise praying in tongues, the more comfortable you will be with it. And as you grow in praying in the spirit, new words and syllables will come forth.

I love what Robert Morris said:

"Babies don't start speaking fluently, and here is the amazing thing…we think it's cute. It doesn't bother us when our children mispronounce words. In the same way, so many people are afraid they aren't going to do it right, but even if you don't do it right your Father likes it. He will like that you are trying."[2]

I have discovered, often, when people get baptized with the Holy Spirit they initially speak in tongues, but afterwards they don't continue to do so. Sometimes they go weeks or even months and never pray in tongues. A person's prayer language will develop and get more expansive the more one prays in the spirit. Many make the mistake of waiting on a "feeling" to overtake them or for the Spirit to come upon them before they pray in tongues again. Remember, you can pray in tongues at any time; you can start it and stop it any time you like. You control it. The more you pray in tongues the easier it is to continue in it.

It is God's will for you to pray in tongues. How do I know that, you ask. Paul said, *"I wish you all spoke in tongues."* (1 Corinthians 14:5a)

Start speaking now!

---

[2] https://www.youtube.com/watch?v=omJ64XuEnMo (4:50)

14

I Was Wrong!

A little girl crawled up into her great grandmother's lap one day. And looking up into her great grandmother's face she saw all those crevices, lines, and wrinkles. Then she felt her own smooth baby-like skin.

She said to her great grandmother, "Did God make you?"

Her great grandmother said, "Yes, honey, God made me."

Then the little girl said, "Well great grandmother, did God make me?"

Her great grandmother said, "Oh yes, dear, God made you, too."

And then the little girl said, "Well great grandmother, don't you think God's doing a lot better job these days?"

It is all about perspective, isn't it? The well meaning little girl looked at all of life through her scope of experience. She innocently assumed all should be like her. Sometimes our understanding is like hers, limited. We see things from a perspective that is narrow and incomplete. I know I did.

Perhaps God has been doing a wonderful job all along, but we just couldn't see it.

As I stated, early in my ministry I enthusiastically preached and taught against the baptism with the Holy Spirit, especially against tongues. I instructed people to stay clear of such erroneous doctrine. The sad part is, I even used the Bible to support my position. Below is a sampling of scriptures that I used to "discredit" the infilling of the Holy Spirit.

My favorite verse to quote was 1 Corinthians 12:13. I used this text to convince my Pentecostal friends that I, as well as all other Baptists, had already experienced the baptism with the Holy Spirit.

"For by one Spirit we were all baptized into one body whether Jews or Greeks, whether slaves or free - and have all been made to drink into one Spirit." (1 Corinthians 12:13)

The standard Baptist position is this: a person receives the fullness of the Spirit at salvation. Period. End of conversation. However, there is a major problem with this logic: it is wrong.

Here is why it is wrong. I focused only on a small portion of the scripture, *"For by one Spirit we were all baptized...."* I stopped and didn't read the rest of the verse. Today, people are making the same mistake I made. They are using the first part of this verse to nullify the necessity and importance of the baptism with the Holy Spirit. However, when you read the whole verse you grasp the total picture and meaning of the passage.

Read the verse again, but this time focus on the emphasized words,

"For by one Spirit we were all baptized INTO ONE BODY...." (1 Corinthians 12:13)

A close look actually reveals this verse is not approving or disproving the teaching regarding the baptism with the Holy Spirit. Rather, it teaches us what the Holy Spirit does for the believer at the moment of their salvation. Take another look: *"For by one Spirit we were all baptized INTO one body...."*

Here is the actual meaning of the verse: immediately upon your conversion, the Holy Spirit immersed you, placed you into the body of Christ. Now, reading the other verses surrounding verse 13, it will make perfect sense to you.

"For as the BODY is one and has many members, but all the members of the ONE BODY, being many, are ONE BODY, so also is Christ. For by one Spirit we were ALL BAPTIZED INTO ONE BODY - whether Jews or Greeks, whether slaves or free - and have all been made to drink into one Spirit. For in fact the BODY is not one member but many." (1 Corinthians 12:12-14)

The context of the above verses deals with the BODY OF CHRIST, not Holy Spirit baptism. This scripture addresses "my placement" INTO the glorious body of Christ. Therefore, anyone who tries to use this passage to discredit the doctrine of the baptism with the Holy Spirit is taking these verses out of context and projecting a line of belief that simply cannot be supported by this text.

Again, here is the irrefutable truth: The precise moment you and I were saved we were immersed, placed, baptized into the body of Christ. We joined the pool of all living believers making up the body of Christ on the earth.

Here is another popular scripture that I once used to try to refute the baptism with the Holy Spirit.

*"One Lord, one faith, **one baptism**..."* (Ephesians 4:5)

Today, many well-meaning Christians assume Paul, in this text, is writing against the fullness of the Holy Spirit; he is not. Why would Paul teach and preach against something he had personally experienced and led others to experience?

On the surface, this verse does seem to defuse the doctrine of the baptism with the Holy Spirit as a subsequent work to salvation. How? Two words, *"one baptism."*

Once again, when you study the context of this passage the true meaning and intent becomes obvious. The Apostle Paul was referring to water baptism. Let me explain.

On one of Paul's journeys to Ephesus, he encountered a group of John the Baptist's disciples. This encounter is mentioned in Acts 19:1-7. We need to familiarize ourselves with this story in order to have a clear understanding of the meaning of *"one baptism."*

"And it happened, while Apollos was at Corinth, that Paul, having passed through the upper regions, came to Ephesus, and finding some disciples. he said to them, 'Did you receive the Holy Spirit when you believed?' So they said to him, 'We have not so much as heard whether there is a Holy Spirit.'

*And he said to them, 'Into what then were you baptized?' So they said, 'Into John's baptism.' Then Paul said, '**John indeed baptized with a baptism of repentance**, saying to the people that they should believe on Him who would come after him, that is on Christ Jesus.' When they heard this, they were baptized in the name of the Lord Jesus."* (Acts 19:1-5)

The meeting Paul had with John's disciples in Ephesus happened close to twenty years after the resurrection of Jesus and the day of Pentecost. Paul quickly discovered they were active followers of John the Baptist and had been **baptized** into John's baptism, which was a baptism of repentance. These precious men were still waiting for the arrival of the Messiah. (Acts 19:4) The text reveals these disciples of John the Baptist had not entered into a personal relationship with Christ. Again, they had only been baptized into John's baptism.

Paul had the blessed privilege of leading these Ephesians to faith in the Lord Jesus, and then baptizing them in the name of Jesus. (v. 50)

This is where it gets interesting. These disciples and perhaps others in Ephesus were baptized into John's baptism, as well as into Jesus' baptism. They had encountered TWO BAPTISMS. It is likely, when Paul wrote, "one baptism" in Ephesians 4:5, that he was emphasizing that John's baptism of repentance had fulfilled its purpose and the new birth baptism in Jesus' name replaced it. In other words, no more need for John's baptism.

However, I am sure there were some at the Church in Ephesus that would not let go of the good ol' days and demanded that they keep emphasizing John's baptism. It became such an issue that Paul wrote them a letter and informed them that only ONE BAPTISM is needed, the baptism in Jesus' name.

117

I admit I was wrong, very wrong. I innocently taught these scriptures incorrectly. I used these texts to embolden my position that the baptism with the Holy Spirit takes place at salvation.

I simply developed my understanding and theology regarding the fullness of the Spirit based upon the thoughts and interpretations of my peers. And when I read these passages as well as others, I saw in the text what I wanted to see. I read them with my mind already made up.

I pray you don't make the same mistake I made.

15

Surprise, Surprise, Surprise!

Benny decided to buy a present for his Uncle Sam's birthday, so with his older brother's help he bought a present, gift wrapped it, and brought it over to his uncle.

His uncle, knowing that Benny's father manufactured apple juice, and seeing a wet spot on the bottom corner of the box, decided to have some fun with Benny by trying to guess what was in the box. "Hmm" said Uncle Sam, touching his finger to the wet spot and taking a quick taste, "I'm going to guess it's a case of apple juice."

"No" said Benny jumping up and down clearly enjoying the game.

"Not apple juice?" asked Uncle Sam, clearly surprised. After another quick taste and a brief pause, he guessed again "Is it apple cider?"

"No," said Benny, practically squealing in excitement "IT'S A PUPPY!"

I love surprises, I really do, but not the kind mentioned above. However, sometimes what we think is in the box isn't what's actually in the box. There is more, much more.

After my wonderful encounter with the Holy Spirit, I discovered that there is more than one baptism in the New Testament. Furthermore, I quickly recognized the Lord wanted me to understand and participate in each one.

I think it is necessary for me to highlight the various types of baptisms mentioned in the New Testament.

Three Baptisms

Baptism #1

"BAPTISM INTO THE BODY OF CHRIST"

As we discovered in the previous chapter, according to the New Testament, at the moment of our salvation experience, we are BAPTIZED INTO Christ and His Body. It is important to note, according to 1 Corinthians 12:13, the **agent** of this baptism **INTO** the body of Christ is the **HOLY SPIRIT**.

*"For as the body is one and has many members, but all the members of that one body, being many, are one body, so also is Christ. For **by one Spirit we were all baptized into one body**—whether Jews or Greeks, whether slaves or free—and have all been made to drink into one Spirit. For in fact the body is not one member but many."* (1 Corinthians 12:12-14)

"Now you are the body of Christ, and members individually." (1 Corinthians 12:27)

*"For you are all sons of God through faith in Christ Jesus. For as many of you as **were baptized into** Christ have put on Christ."* (Galatians 3:26-27)

Again, as a reference point, the Holy Spirit is the one who baptizes us into the body of Christ.

Baptism #2

"BAPTISM IN WATER"

The Bible teaches that water baptism is an outward demonstration of a believer's faith in the Lord Jesus. This act of obedience visually demonstrates the believer's death to sin, the burial of the old life, and the beginning of new life in Christ. (Romans 6:3, 4) After one's conversion, this baptism should take place as soon as possible. The agent of this baptism is a minister, another disciple, or a Christian friend.

*"Go therefore and make disciples of all nations **BAPTIZING** them in the name of the Father and of the Son and of the Holy Spirit."* (Matthew 28:19)

*"Then Peter said to them, "Repent, and **let every one of you be baptized** in the name of Jesus Christ ...."* (Acts 2:3)

121

*"Now as they went down the road, they came to some water. And the eunuch said, '**See, here is water. What hinders me from being baptized?**' Then Philip said, 'If you believe with all your heart, you may.' And he answered and said, 'I believe that Jesus Christ is the Son of God.' So he commanded the chariot to stand still. And **both Philip and the eunuch went down into the water, and he baptized him.**"* (Acts 8:36-38)

Baptism #3

"THE BAPTISM WITH THE HOLY SPIRIT"

Among other events, such as the death, burial and resurrection of Jesus, **the baptism with the Holy Spirit** is mentioned in each of the four gospels.

I find this extraordinary and meaningful. Let me say it again,

The baptism with the Holy Spirit is mentioned in **ALL** four of the gospels. Did you know that?

The language is specific and leaves no doubt of Jesus' intention and desire for each believer, not just the first disciples.

Each referenced verse identifies Jesus as the agent who baptizes believers with the Holy Spirit.

John the Baptist:

*"I indeed baptize you with water unto repentance, but He who is coming after me is mightier than I, whose sandals I am not worthy to carry. **He (Jesus) will BAPTIZE you WITH the HOLY SPIRIT and FIRE.**"* (Matthew 3:11)

*"I indeed baptized you with water, but **He (Jesus) will baptize you with the Holy Spirit**."* (Mark 1:8)

*"John answered, saying to all, 'I indeed baptize you with water; but One mightier than I is coming, whose sandal strap I am not worthy to loose. **He (Jesus) will baptize you with the Holy Spirit and fire.**'"* (Luke 3:16)

*"I did not know Him, but He who sent me to baptize with water said to me, 'Upon whom you see the Spirit descending, and remaining on Him, **this is He (Jesus) who baptizes with the Holy Spirit.**'"* (John 1:33)

The Bible is unmistakable about the value and importance of the baptism with the Holy Spirit. Again, this experience is specifically mentioned four times in the first four books of the New Testament. You may ask, what is the significance of its repeated emphasis? From the beginning, the precedent was being set - it reveals God's intent that every believer should be baptized with the Holy Spirit and fire, no exceptions!

Furthermore, God wanted to communicate to His Church that Holy Spirit baptism should not be minimized or neglected in any way.

*"For John truly baptized with water, **BUT** you shall be **BAPTIZED WITH THE HOLY SPIRIT** not many days from now."* (Acts 1:5)

*"And they all were **FILLED WITH THE HOLY SPIRIT** and began to speak in tongues, as the Spirit gave them utterance."* (Acts 2:4)

All three baptisms are of utmost importance. With that being said, the first baptism is by the Holy Spirit. You have no control over it; it takes place at your conversion. However, you determine if you will participate in the other two baptisms. Let me add, both the second and third baptisms are available to all of His disciples and are presented to us as commands, not suggestions.

I know this may sound harsh but it is true: Your refusal or resistance to participate in the second and third baptisms will drastically affect your walk with Christ.

You may be thinking you don't need the third baptism, baptism with the Holy Spirit. You feel all is fine and that your walk with God is great.

It may be wonderful, but you don't know what you don't know.

Let me explain.

You don't know how much better it could be because you haven't yet experienced the fullness of the Holy Spirit. You are only experiencing a fraction of what God has for you.

16

I Got It All When I Got Saved!

Before my dramatic encounter with the Holy Spirit, I distinctly remember, on more than one occasion, people asking me if I had been baptized with the Holy Spirit. Every time I responded with a resounding "Yes!" Then they would ask a follow-up question, "When did it happen and where?" Here was my reaction, "At the moment I got saved!"

Make no mistake about it, when you are saved at that precise moment the Holy Spirit comes to live on the inside of you; the Spirit of God takes up residence in your body.

"Or do you not know that your body is the temple of the Holy Spirit who is in you…." (1 Corinthians 6:19)

He indwells you. In fact, it is impossible to be born again without the Spirit of God inside of you.

However, it is one thing for the Spirit to indwell you and quite another for the Spirit to baptize, saturate, overcome and fill you to overflowing. There is a distinct difference in the two experiences; a night and day difference.

I don't want you to be confused, so let me share with you how the Holy Spirit works in a person's life before and after they are born again.

Before we were saved the Holy Spirit was **WITH** us, *"convicting us of sin, righteousness and judgment."* (John 16:8) It didn't matter where we were: the bar, work, kitchen table or church, the Spirit was constantly reminding us we needed to get right with God, to be saved.

Many of us can reflect back and vividly recall the Spirit drawing us this way. At precise moments, the Spirit of God would reveal to us how our sin had separated us from a loving Father and how that same loving Father desired to have a personal relationship with us.

When we finally repented of our sin and invited Jesus to take over our life, at that moment the Holy Spirit came **INTO** us. *"...for He dwells with you and will be in you."* (John 14:17) The Holy Spirit, at conversion, resides within every true believer.

When we responded in obedience and yielded to the baptism with the Holy Spirit, the Spirit of God came **UPON** us. "You shall receive power after the Holy Spirit COMES UPON you...." (Acts 1:8)

Look at the progression: "WITH," "IN," "UPON." This has been God's plan for His followers since the beginning. The question is, have you experienced all three workings of the Spirit?

Most believers have experienced the first two, and far too many have yet to have Him come "upon" them - in other words, to be baptized with the Holy Spirit. The reason for this is, we were and are being taught wrong. I was.

I Was Taught Wrong (I believed wrong, too)

I was taught that when the Holy Spirit came on the "day of Pentecost" (the Upper Room encounter, Acts 2), this was the initial coming of the Holy Spirit, and that is correct. However, I was also led to believe what actually happened in the Upper Room wasn't normative, nor was it to be duplicated in our day. Therefore, I was instructed that I should not and need not seek such an experience.

God's gift is one thing; our appropriation of that gift is quite another."

Furthermore, it was strongly communicated to me that the experience recorded in Acts 2 does not need to be repeated because, at the moment of my salvation, I received the baptism with the Holy Spirit.

I was shocked when I discovered that A. J. Gordon, an influential Baptist minister who lived in the 19th century, made the following statement regarding what takes place at the moment of someone's conversion and what needs to happen afterward.

127

"The baptism of the Holy Spirit was given once and for all on the day of Pentecost, when the Paraclete came in person to make His abode in the church. But that does not mean that every believer has received the baptism. God's gift is one thing; our appropriation of that gift is quite another."[3]

He continued, "It seems clear from the Scripture that it is still the duty and privilege of believers to receive the Holy Spirit by a conscious, definite act of appropriating faith, just as they received Jesus Christ."[4]

Gordon also commented about Acts 2:4, *"And they were all filled with the Holy Spirit."* He said, "What is spoken here seems nothing different from what in other scriptures is called the 'reception of the Spirit,' an act seemingly distinct from the 'sealing of the Spirit.' It is a transaction that may be repeated, and will be if we are living in the Spirit. But it is clearly an experience belonging to one who has already been converted.

"This is clearly evidenced in the life of Paul. If the reception of the Spirit is associated always and inseparably with conversion, one will reasonably ask why a conversion so marked and so radical as that of the Apostle Paul need be followed by such an experience as that named in Acts 19:17: *'And Ananias went his way and entered into the house; and putting his hands on him said, "Brother Saul, the Lord, even Jesus, that appeared to you in the way as has sent me that you might receive your sight and be filled with the Holy Spirit."'* Here we find a divine something distinct from

---

[3] A. J. Gordon, The Ministry of the Spirit, p. 55.
[4] ibid

conversion and subsequent to it, which we have called the 'reception of the Spirit.'"[5]

He added, "It seems to me beyond question as a matter of experience both of Christians in the present day and of the early church, as recorded by inspiration, that in addition to the gift of the Spirit received by the apostles at Pentecost - a blessing to be asked for and expected by Christians still, and be described in language similar to that employed in the book of Acts."[6]

When I read his writings on the Holy Spirit, my spirit leapt on the inside of me. I couldn't believe what I was reading, a well known Baptist minister and respected scholar validating the baptism with the Holy Spirit as something to experience after one's conversion. This was revolutionary!

No Not One

There is not one – no, not one - scripture in the New Testament that contextually supports the position that you automatically receive Holy Spirit baptism at conversion. This viewpoint is based on assumption and opinion.

Furthermore, no passage forbids us from having an Upper Room experience with the Holy Spirit. I have searched thoroughly through the New Testament to find such texts and there are none. On the contrary, the Bible consistently thrusts us forward and encourages us to pursue the baptism with the Holy Spirit.

---

[5] ibid
[6] A. J. Gordon, The Ministry of the Spirit, pp. 65, 66.

In my quest to know the truth regarding the baptism with the Holy Spirit, I quickly realized that what happened in Acts 2 is not a "one-time-only" event. However, professionally, I was trained that it was a single "moment in time" and that this Holy Spirit outpouring shouldn't and couldn't be repeated.

The reasoning of those who taught me was that the Upper Room encounter was the initial coming of the Holy Spirit to the Church; therefore, it was necessary for "it" to happen in such a grandiose way in order to launch the church forward in power.

We were - and even people today are - taught that in no way is this type of encounter to be expected to repeat itself. In other words, what took place in Acts 2 wasn't to be the new norm, or repeated, but rather an anomaly, a one-time event.

> When I got saved, I experienced the benefit of Christ's death, even though His crucifixion took place over 2,000 years ago.

Yes, the *day* of Pentecost itself can never be repeated. I agree; "that day" has come and gone. It is history. But the experience, results and manifestations that occurred on that day can happen again. In fact it did.

In the book of Acts, we find the Holy Spirit falling upon people many years later in the exact same way He did in the Upper Room, and in one case, Acts 19, it happened two decades removed from the day of Pentecost.

Let me legitimize my position by using Jesus' death on the cross. It is a fact that the **day** of Christ's crucifixion cannot be repeated. However, today, I can access and apply to my life what Christ did for me on the cross.

When I got saved, I experienced the benefit of Christ's death, even though His crucifixion took place over 2,000 years ago. By faith, I acquired what happened at Calvary and made it mine. I personalized it. I took it as my own. I tapped into His provision for salvation.

The outpouring of the Holy Spirit on the day of Pentecost also set something into motion that is still available today for every believer. Even though we are 2,000 years removed from it, by faith we can appropriate it for our own lives.

I did and it changed everything.

"...and you shall receive the gift of the Holy Spirit. **For the promise is to you and to your children, and to all who are afar off,** *as many as the Lord our God will call."* (Acts 2:38,39)

17

Why Not
In The
Epistles?

As a Southern Baptist pastor I had often asked myself this question, "If the baptism with the Holy Spirit is such an important event, why didn't Paul or Peter write about it in the other books of the New Testament?"

The absence of any mention of Holy Spirit baptism in the epistles seemed to support the argument I used that the experience in Acts 2 was a one-time event. My position was, if God wanted us to be baptized with the Holy Spirit the same way the early disciples were, then He would have left us further instructions.

Early on in my ministerial training, I was taught not to develop and/or build a theology of the Holy Spirit from the book of Acts. The reasoning? The book of Acts is a historical narrative and is classified as a transitional book, descriptive in nature, but not to be used for developing beneficial doctrine.

Therefore, I developed my functional doctrine from the epistles. I drew the conclusion that, since the baptism with the Holy Spirit was not mentioned or referred to in the epistles, I was bound not to accept it as an "ongoing" New Testament experience.

I ignored the book of Acts all together when it came time to formulate my doctrinal belief on the Holy Spirit. However, NOW I KNOW you can develop usable doctrine from the book of Acts.

In 2 Timothy 3:16 we read, *"**ALL** scripture is given by inspiration of God, and is **PROFITABLE FOR DOCTRINE.…"***

This passage includes the book of Acts!

It is true that the fullness of the Holy Spirit is not mentioned in any of the epistles outside the book of Ephesians. And only in one verse, 5:18, does Paul tell the believers to *"be filled with the Spirit."*

Let's dig deeper into the idea that the book of Acts cannot be used to develop correct and profitable doctrine.

If we deny the validity of the baptism with the Holy Spirit because it is not mentioned in the epistles then we possibly could deny the doctrine of salvation as well.

What?

Yes! If scholars use the above argument for the denial of Holy Spirit baptism, then we must be consistent and use the same reasoning for the doctrine of salvation.

In my study of the Bible, outside of the books of Acts, Romans and Ephesians, we are not told HOW TO BE SAVED or given a CLEAR PLAN OF SALVATION in the epistles. If this is true, then we must say that God doesn't want us to experience salvation because it goes unmentioned in all but two of the epistles.

One might say, "Well, there are plenty of other scriptures in the New Testament that tell us we need to be saved." You are correct and I wholeheartedly agree. But, I must add, there are plenty of passages outside the epistles that validate and support teaching of Holy Spirit baptism as well.

> ...the book of Acts has no less than five examples of individuals and groups of people who received the baptism with the Holy Spirit **after** their salvation experience.

In each of the gospels, the baptism with the Holy Spirit is mentioned - not only mentioned, but points out that Jesus Himself will baptize us with the Holy Spirit. (Matthew 3:11, Mark 1:8, Luke 3:16, John 1:33)

Plus, the book of Acts has no less than five examples of individuals and groups of people who received the baptism with the Holy Spirit **after** their salvation experience. (Acts 2; Acts 8; Acts 9; Acts 10; Acts 19) These experiences were documented, and occurred even decades after the initial outpouring of the Holy Spirit in the Upper Room, thus, setting a historical precedent that this encounter with the Holy Spirit was to never cease.

In my opinion, there is a simple explanation why the doctrines of the baptism with the Holy Spirit and plan of salvation are not repeated in the epistles. The apostles Paul, Peter, John and other writers of the New Testament were writing letters of encouragement to the newly birthed churches. The people in the churches they were addressing were already saved and on their way to heaven; furthermore, those same people had already experienced Holy Spirit baptism. It was "just understood" that after one was saved, the very next step was to be "baptized with the Spirit." (Examples: Samaritans in Acts 8:17; Paul in Acts 9:17; Cornelius in Acts 10:44; Acts 19:6)

There was absolutely no doubt or confusion involved. They simply followed the examples set for them. This is why Paul said to the disciples of John in Acts 19:2, *"Have you RECEIVED the Holy Spirit since you believed?"* Paul clearly understood the pattern and knew the importance of being empowered by the Holy Spirit. I find it interesting that it was the FIRST QUESTION he asked.

The writers of the New Testament did not find it necessary to address the issues of salvation and the baptism with the Holy Spirit in every letter. According to the book of Hebrews, these foundational teachings were elementary issues that had already been resolved and seen as staples within the church. Moreover, the writer encouraged his readers to leave such doctrines and go on to maturity in the Lord.

*"Therefore, leaving the discussion of the elementary principles of Christ, let us go on to perfection, **not laying again the foundation of repentance from dead works and of faith toward God,** of the **doctrine of baptisms,** of*

laying on of hands, of resurrection of the dead, and of eternal judgment." (Hebrews 6:1-2)

Let me help you understand it more clearly by giving you a contemporary scenario. If I were to teach a Bible class on the subject of "personal sanctification," I would not spend time teaching about how to be saved. I would assume all the people in attendance were born again. I would move on and deal with issues at hand, such as sanctification. Just because I don't directly address the issue of salvation, it doesn't mean that is not a necessity or a genuine experience. Simply, there would be no need for me to teach them about salvation because I am addressing believers who have already had the new birth experience.

Here is a biblical example of what I mean. Earlier in this chapter, I referenced the Apostle Paul and his engagement with twelve of John's disciples in Acts 19. Paul quickly discovered they were not born again and led them to faith in Christ and then he baptized them in water. (Acts 19:5)

Look at the very next thing Paul does: *"...he laid hands on them and the Holy Spirit **CAME UPON** them and they spoke in tongues and prophesied."* (Acts 19:6)

Their experience was almost identical to the Upper Room encounter even though it occurred approximately twenty years later.

Three years after the Acts 19 episode, Paul wrote the book of Ephesians to the believers dwelling in Ephesus. I conclude that it was not necessary to specifically address the baptism with the Holy Spirit. Why? The church at Ephesus had already experienced the baptism with the Holy Spirit. It was a staple of the early church, a foundational doctrine. However, Paul highlighted the importance and necessity of staying filled with the Holy Spirit. (Ephesians 5:18)

I hope my explanations have removed another obstacle that has been keeping you from experiencing the baptism with the Holy Spirit. For some of you, the journey to this blessed encounter will take some time and further explanation. Keep researching and studying; the truth will set you free.

Let's continue to press toward the deeper life!

Section Three

"Sources Of Authority"

18

Not A Bronze Medalist

Miscommunication is one of the leading causes for misinformation and misunderstanding within an organization, family and even a church. If an instruction or an idea isn't clearly and effectively communicated, it makes things complicated and breeds confusion. Regretfully, I know this firsthand. I have been on both sides of the miscommunication nightmare.

For example, nothing hurts a corporate brand like failing to accurately communicate your purpose and message. Throughout the years we have been treated to some funny misinterpretations due to not communicating well. Here are a few of those legendary miscues.

- The name Coca-Cola in China was first rendered as *Ke-kou-ke-la*. While doing the research for suitable characters, the employees found that a number of shopkeepers had also been looking for Chinese equivalents for Coca-Cola. Unfortunately, the Coke Company did not discover that the phrase means, "Bite the wax tadpole" or "Female horse stuffed with wax." Coke then researched 40,000 Chinese characters and found a close phonetic equivalent, *"ko-kou-ko-le,"* which can be loosely translated as: "Happiness in the mouth."[7]

- In 1987, Colonel Sanders introduced its first Kentucky Fried Chicken store in China. The slogan, "Finger-lickin' good," came out as: "Eat your fingers off."[8]

- In Taiwan, the translation of the Pepsi slogan: "Come alive with the Pepsi Generation" came out as "Pepsi will bring your ancestors back from the dead."

- Clairol, a division of Procter and Gamble, in 2006 introduced its "Mist Stick" curling iron to the German market; then discovered that "mist" is slang for manure.[9]

Shiv Khera, an Indian author, offered this advice: "Avoid miscommunication. The price you pay for it is horrendous."

I agree.

---

[7] https://www.coca-colacompany.com/stories/bite-the-wax-ta
[8] http://www.languageresources.com/blunders.html
[9] https://thelanguagefactory.co.uk/translations-go-bad/

Charles F. Glassman got it right when he said, "Miscommunication leads to misunderstanding, which rarely leads to anything good."

As you can see from the above examples, poor communication can be costly, disastrous and cause one to have an unintentional setback in plans. The companies meant well, but grossly miscommunicated.

Charles F. Glassman got it right when he said, "Miscommunication leads to misunderstanding, which rarely leads to anything good."

Below are two mistakes the church has made over the years when addressing and explaining the Holy Spirit. To some, these mistakes may not mean much, but I believe over time the miscommunication has had a detrimental effect upon the Church and has confused many.

1. The Holy Spirit - "Third Person of the Trinity"

Have you ever heard someone refer to the Holy Spirit as the "third person of the Trinity?"

I have and it deeply troubles me.

In the early years of my walk with Jesus, I heard Bible teachers and pastors refer to the Holy Spirit as the "third" member of the Trinity. After hearing this phrase repeated over and over, I subconsciously developed a not-so-healthy opinion of the Holy Spirit.

Because of the terminology used, I started looking at the Holy Spirit as somewhat inferior. He was labeled "third," which I subconsciously translated as, not as important as the other two.

Nowhere in Scripture is the Holy Spirit even remotely labeled the "third member of the Trinity."

I don't know about you, but when I hear someone say "third person in the Trinity," my mind immediately thinks third-place, bronze medalist, or white ribbon holder. Not 1st, not 2nd, but 3rd!

Nowhere in Scripture is the Holy Spirit even remotely labeled the "third member of the Trinity." You can't find it; it's not there.

So why does this term exist? Where did it come from? Scholars and Church leaders, without authority from Scripture, have loosely classified the Holy Spirit as the third component of the Trinity. In fairness, I believe it was an innocent attempt by well-meaning people to categorize the Spirit's position in the Godhead. So in an attempt to make things easier to understand, each member of the Trinity got a number. For many people, the number three suggests the last in line.

Men have unintentionally minimized the Holy Spirit's role and value.

Because of this classification, the Holy Spirit is mostly, if not altogether, ignored by many Christian denominations and movements. Sadly, He has become the forgotten member of the Trinity. For that reason, too many Christians know very little about Him. Why? He is third.

Moving forward we have to change our language. We can no longer inappropriately label and underemphasize the role of the Holy Spirit.

2. The Holy Spirit Is "SOMEONE" Not "Something"

In scripture the Holy Spirit is never referred to as an "it," an "outside force" or an "unknown essence." He is referred to as a Person.

I have to be honest, I cringe and basically break out in hives every time I hear the Holy Spirit referred to as an "it."

On multiple occasions, Jesus spoke about the Holy Spirit and the role He would have in the disciples' lives. Every time, He referred to the Spirit as a Person. This is best highlighted in Jesus' prayer in John 14 where, six times, Jesus used a personal pronoun referencing the Holy Spirit.

*"And I will ask the Father, and He will give you another Counselor to be with you forever. **He** is the Spirit of truth. The world is unable to receive **Him** because it doesn't see **Him** or know **Him**. But you do know **Him**, because **He** remains with you and will be in you."* (John 14:16-17)

Below is a short list of other examples that substantiate the Holy Spirit's ministry and role in the lives of believers, not as an "essence" but a Person.

The Holy Spirit:

Speaks (Acts 8:29)

Empowers (Acts 1:8)

Makes decisions (Acts (15:28)

Can be grieved (Eph. 4:30)

Counsels (John 16:8)

Can be lied to (Acts 5:3-4)

Distributes the spiritual gifts (1 Cor. 12:11)

Guides (John 116:13)

Bears witness (Acts 5:32)

Baptizes (1 Corinthians 12:13)

Groans, prays, and intercedes (Romans 8:26-27)

Helps us (Rom. 8:26-27)

Sometimes prevents our plans (Acts 16:6-7)

Comforts (John 15:26)

Teaches (John 14:26)

All of the activities listed above are not the work of an "it," but of the Holy Spirit. He is a fully functioning member of the Godhead and is active in accomplishing the Father's will.

Dr. A. J. Gordon tells of a Welsh preacher who, having been scheduled to preach one night, asked to be allowed to withdraw for a time before the service. He remained in seclusion so long that the good man of the house sent his servant to request him to come and meet the waiting congregation. As she came near the room, she heard what seemed to be an indication of conversation between two parties, and though in subdued tone of voice, she caught the words, "I will not go unless You go with me."

Without interfering, she returned and reported, "He will come all right, and the Other will come, too." And sure enough, when he came, the Other One came along, and with such power that it proved a wonderful service in which many found newness of life.[10]

"Without the Spirit of God, we can do nothing. We are as ships without the wind, branches without sap, and like coals without fire; we are useless." These are the words of the infamous Charles Spurgeon.

It is of utmost importance that we get to know the Holy Spirit and the value of His ministry. We must tap into the deep well of the Spirit of God, honor Him and elevate Him to His rightful place. In doing so, the Spirit of God will show up in our lives with unprecedented power.

---

[10] Christian Union Herald - (http://www.moreillustrations.com/Illustrations/holy%20spirit%201. html)

My goal in the pages that follow is to effectively communicate how you can experience the fullness of the Holy Spirit in your life.

My approach will be methodical and intentional as I unpack the riches of a Spirit-filled life.

19

Heroes Of The Faith

Do the names Moody, Finney, Spurgeon, Carmichael, Chambers, Judson, Gordon, Tozer, Smith, Murray and Whitefield mean anything to you? While I was in college and seminary, we studied their ministries and were encouraged to emulate them. Indeed, they were great examples of faith, holiness and power!

When my professors would speak about these men, my heartbeat would quicken. I listened with holy jealousy; I yearned to be used by God the way they were used. When I graduated from seminary to begin my first pastorate, I was determined to preach like Finney and win souls like Moody.

It didn't take long to realize I wasn't measuring up. I was falling well short of what I expected. The more I failed, the more I tried. I worked harder and longer. I surrendered more and more and even studied and prayed more often. Yet, regardless of how much I worked, studied, prayed and yielded, I wasn't manifesting the same fruit they manifested.

Someone Forgot To Tell Me

My professors and teachers told me about all the wonderful things the individuals above did, but they forgot to tell me the key to their success. NO ONE took the time to tell me their secret.

Guess what? I found out what their secret was - the baptism with the Holy Spirit!

Read carefully as the heroes of the faith share their thoughts on the baptism with the Holy Spirit.

DWIGHT LYMAN MOODY

Dwight L. Moody was a dynamic soul-winner. He was energetic, assertive and his passion was to introduce people to Jesus. He preached with great fervency to large and small audiences here in America and abroad.

An elderly man was first to confront Moody about the absence of God's anointing on his ministry. Moody was on his way to New York when the man pointed his finger at him and said, "Young man, when you speak again, honor the Holy Ghost."

God had a precise message He wanted to get to Moody. In Chicago, there were two precious ladies who attended

Moody's meetings. These women became greatly burdened for Moody and wanted him to be filled with the Spirit. They brazenly approached him after one of the meetings and said, "We have been praying for you." Moody responded to their declaration, "Why don't you pray for the people?" Undistracted by his response, they sternly answered, "You need power." Moody shot back, "I need power? Why, I thought I had power."

These two encounters challenged and deeply moved Moody.

One day in New York, Moody experienced for himself the fullness of the Holy Spirit. He described his encounter with the Spirit of God this way, "I had such an experience of His love that I had to ask Him to stay His hand."

> "The Holy Ghost coming upon them with power is **distinct and separate from conversion**. If the Scripture doesn't teach it, I am ready to correct it."
> D. L. Moody

After his baptism with the Holy Spirit he said, "The sermons were not different; I did not present any new truths, and yet hundreds were converted. I would not now be placed back where I was before that blessed experience if you should give me all the world. It would be as the small dust of the balance."

Moody was scriptural in his teaching on his experience. He said, "Now I want this thing clearly understood. We believe firmly that if any man … has been cleansed by the blood, redeemed by the blood and been sealed by the Holy Ghost, the Holy Ghost dwells in him." He added, "The Holy Ghost coming upon them with power is **distinct and separate**

from conversion. If the Scripture doesn't teach it, I am ready to correct it."

He believed that Peter, James, John and the other disciples were saved, but did not have power. He said, "...they were saints without power, and must tarry in Jerusalem until imbued with power from on high. I believe we should accomplish more in one week than we should in years if we had only this fresh baptism...."

Dr. C. I. Scofield, editor of the Scofield Reference Bible, spoke at Moody's funeral service. In part he said, "The secrets to Dwight L. Moody's power were: First, he had a definite experience with Christ's saving grace. Secondly, he believed in the divine authority of the Scriptures. The Bible was to him the voice of God, and he made it resound as such in the consciences of men. Thirdly, he was baptized with the Holy Spirit, and he knew it. It was to him as definite an experience as his conversion...."[11]

OSWALD CHAMBERS

Many people are acquainted with Chambers' classic devotional guide, "My Utmost For His Highest." Chambers has left us a legacy of thoughts, truths and meditations. We are forever indebted to his contribution to the body of Christ.

"...THIS THING IS A FRAUD" - Chambers

When one reads the life history of Oswald Chambers one quickly realizes not all was well in the early years of his walk with God. While attending Dunoon College, he became desperate for the fullness of God. He said, "I knew no one who had what I wanted; in fact I did not know what I did

---

[11] V. Raymond Edman, They Found the Secret, pp. 73-78.

want, but I knew that if what I had was all the Christianity there was, the thing was a fraud. Then Luke 11:13 got hold of me: *'If ye then, being evil, know how to give good gifts to your children, how much more shall your heavenly Father give the Holy Spirit to them that ask Him?'"*

He added, "But how could I, bad motivated as I was, possibly ask for the gift of the Holy Spirit? Then it was borne in upon me that I had to claim the gift from God on the authority of Jesus Christ and testify to having done so."

Shortly thereafter, Oswald Chambers received the baptism with the Holy Spirit by faith. This experience impacted his life so much that on his tombstone is a portion of one of his favorite verses, Luke 11:13, *"How much more will your Heavenly Father give the Holy Spirit to them that ask Him?"*[12]

ANDREW MURRAY

On the surface, all seemed well; however, deep in his soul Andrew Murray knew something wasn't right. Even though he was having success in ministry he still had a growing emptiness.

Read his own words as he describes his condition: "All the time, there was a burning in my heart, a dissatisfaction and restlessness inexpressible...I remember in my little room at Bloemfontein how I used to sit and think. What is the matter? Here I am, knowing that God has justified me in the blood of Christ, but I have no power for service."

Andrew Murray did the right thing; he set his mind to receive the baptism with the Holy Spirit. Murray added, "When once

---

[12] V. Raymond Edman, They Found The Secret, pp. 31-37.

the distinct recognition of what the indwelling of the Spirit was meant to bring is brought home to the soul, and is ready to give up all to be made partaker of it, the believer may ask and expect what may be termed a baptism of the Spirit."

He felt God gave him more and more of His blessed Spirit. He further commented that this experience will lift the person to a different level from the one on which he was living.[13]

CHARLES G. FINNEY

Here was a man possessed by God, a powerful preacher and an astute student of the Bible. Very few, if any, could rival Charles Finney's ability to preach the Word of God. Even today many want to know what his secret was.

Read carefully the testimony that follows. In his own words he details what made the difference.

One day after pouring his heart before the Lord, Finney said, "I received a mighty baptism of the Holy Ghost. The Holy Spirit

"These waves came over me, and over me, and over me, one after the other, until I cried out, 'I shall die if these waves continue to pass over me. Lord, I cannot bear anymore.'" Charles Finney

descended upon me in a manner that seemed to go through me, body and soul. I could feel the impression, like a wave of electricity, going through and through me. Indeed, it seemed to come in waves and waves of liquid love, for I could not

---

[13] A. J. Gordon, The Ministry of the Holy Spirit, p. 54.

express it in any other way. It seemed like the very breath of God. I can recollect distinctly that it seemed to fan me, like immense wings."

He added, "No words can express the wonderful love that was shed abroad in my heart ... I literally bellowed out the unutterable gushings of my heart. These waves came over me, and over me, and over me, one after the other, until I cried out, 'I shall die if these waves continue to pass over me. Lord, I cannot bear anymore.'"[14]

Finney's baptism with the Holy Spirit changed his life forever. It marked him. He became a man of prayer and power. He preached like few others; he had both unction and power. He may have been America's greatest evangelist.

And what was the key? The difference in his life and ministry was the baptism with the Holy Spirit.

CHARLES SPURGEON

Spurgeon definitely believed that each believer should experience the fullness of God. In response to Paul's encounter with the disciples from Ephesus, in Acts 19:2, Spurgeon asked three questions. One, "Did you receive Him when you believed?" Two, "Have you received since you believed?" Third, "Are you daily receiving Him as you believe?"

Spurgeon encouraged believers everywhere to "drink in" the Holy Spirit every morning and to welcome Him each day.

Over the years I have heard countless people say, "When you get saved, you receive all the Holy Spirit you are ever

---

[14] V. Raymond Edman, They Found The Secret, pp. 38-47.

going to receive." Years ago, Spurgeon addressed this belief, "All believers have more room for the Holy Spirit in their lives. If anyone has the idea that he cannot have any more grace, I am afraid he is especially in need of it."

Concerning the Holy Spirit, Spurgeon said, "He that has much grace and is filled with the Spirit of God shall have two heavens - a heaven here and a heaven hereafter. He who has the Spirit richly shall have the joy of the Lord as his strength and the joy of the Lord hereafter to be his reward. Come, let us ask for all that God is willing to give. Does He not say, 'Open thy mouth wide, and I will fill it?' Come, little one, why remain little? Come. You are living on crumbs; why not eat abundantly of the bread of heaven? Do not be content with the pennies when a king's ransom is at your disposal. Poor brother, rise out of your poverty. Sister, bowed down by reason of the little of the Spirit of God you have received, believe for more and pray upon a larger scale. May the Lord enlarge your heart and fill it and then enlarge it again and fill it again, so that from day to day we may receive the Holy Ghost, till at the last, Jesus shall receive us into His glory."[15]

Some of God's choicest and greatest servants believed in the baptism with the Holy Spirit. They experienced firsthand the fruit that baptism produced and then encouraged others to follow their footsteps.

---

[15] Charles Spurgeon, <u>What the Holy Spirit Does In A Believer's Life,</u> pp. 114-115.

20

Is The Baptism With The Holy Spirit Biblical?

Have you ever bought something that, until the time of the purchase, you rarely saw in public?

For example, a car. You finally decided to get this really cool car and you thought you would be the only one on the road who has it. But, as soon as you pulled out of the dealership, you saw that same type of car everywhere.

The same thing happened to me with the baptism of the Hoy Spirit. The more I studied this subject the more I started seeing it in the Bible; it started popping up everywhere.

When I started reading the New Testament without my denominational glasses on, I was shocked to find so many passages and examples regarding the infilling of the Holy Spirit. I am not the only one who discovered a whole new portion of the Bible.

One friend who happened to be the son of a Baptist minister said, "I can't believe I've missed those scriptures before." He added, "Todd, I started reading the Bible without those denominational glasses you talked about and it all became so clear."

The very same thing can happen to you when you approach the Word of God with no bias and no presuppositions.

I quickly discovered that the Bible gives us example after example of people who encountered the fullness of God. Each of them experienced a baptism of power. They entered into that sweet life, a life characterized by anointing, power, boldness, consistency and holiness. We should learn from them and follow their pattern.

JESUS

This is amazing: before Jesus began His public ministry, He prayed and waited for the anointing and power of the Holy Spirit to come upon Him, in Luke 3:21b-22:

*"Jesus also being baptized, and **praying**, the heaven was opened, and the Holy Spirit descended in a bodily shape like a dove upon Him."*

I know what you are thinking, "What makes you think He was praying for the Holy Spirit to descend upon Him?" The prophet Isaiah under the direction of God gave many prophetic words concerning the Messiah, two of which are:

(1) *"And the spirit of the Lord shall rest upon Him, the spirit of wisdom and understanding, the spirit of counsel and might, the spirit of knowledge and of the fear of the Lord."* (Isaiah 11:2)

(2) *"The Spirit of the LORD is upon me, because the LORD has anointed me to preach good tidings to the poor. He has sent me to heal the broken hearted, to proclaim liberty to the captives and the opening of the prison to those who are bound; 2. To proclaim the acceptable year of the Lord, and the day of vengeance of our God; to comfort all who mourn."* (Isaiah 61:1-2)

I am convinced Jesus was praying for these verses to become a reality in His life. It was His time to begin His public ministry and He knew He needed God's enabling power to work in, on and through Him. The scriptures undeniably communicate that in order for Jesus to have been able to fulfill His ministry, He had to have the empowerment of the Holy Spirit.

"And the Holy Spirit descended on Him in bodily form like a dove. And a voice came from heaven: 'You are my Son, whom I love; with you I am well pleased.'" (Luke 3:22)

"Jesus, FULL of the Holy Spirit, returned from the Jordan and was led by the Spirit in the desert." (Luke 4:1)

After His baptism, He was led by the Spirit into the wilderness where He fasted for forty days. Upon ending His season of fasting we see the position and value of the Holy Spirit upon His life.

"Then Jesus returned in the power of the Spirit to Galilee, and news of Him went out through all the surrounding region." (Luke 4:14)

Note, the Bible says the Holy Spirit descended upon Jesus LIKE a dove; it wasn't an actual dove. The picture the writer wanted us to capture is the Holy Spirit came down upon and rested and remained upon Jesus.

With the Holy Spirit coming upon Jesus, God openly revealed to His followers how the people of God should operate and fulfill the Father's will on the earth. By this action God clearly displayed a vital kingdom principle.

My friend, let me say something to you that may startle you. All that Jesus did on the earth was accomplished as a result of the ministry of Holy Spirit in and through Him.

For example, every crippled person that was made to walk, every demonized person liberated, each individual raised from the dead, every blind eye made to see, deaf ear made to hear and every other miracle Jesus performed was accomplished through the ongoing ministry of the Holy Spirit upon His life.

Jesus thoroughly understood the value and role the Spirit of God had in His life and He relied on the power of God to manifest through Him.

Jesus said it Himself, *"I cast out devils by the Spirit of God."* (Matthew 12:28)

He added, *"I can of Myself do nothing...."* (John 5:30)

In Acts 10:38, we really do find the secret to His success:

*"How God **ANOINTED** Jesus of Nazareth **with the Holy Spirit** and power, and how He went around doing good and healing all who were under the power of the devil **BECAUSE** God was **WITH** Him."*

Here is my assessment so far, and I hope you agree with me.

If Jesus, the Son of the Living God, needed the Holy Spirit to come upon Him to be successful in doing the Father's work, how much more do you and I need the same endowment of power?

> John the Baptist even prophesied that a significant part of Jesus' ministry would be to baptize His followers with the Holy Spirit.

It would be devastating to think we could do ministry without the Holy Spirit upon us. Jesus knew how catastrophic it would be, so before He ascended to heaven, He instructed His disciples to go and tarry until they were empowered by the Holy Spirit (Luke 24:49) - the same Spirit that enabled Him to fulfill the Father's plans.

John the Baptist even prophesied that a significant part of Jesus' ministry would be to baptize His followers with the Holy Spirit.

*"I indeed baptize you with water unto repentance: but He that comes after me is mightier than I ... **He shall baptize you WITH THE HOLY SPIRIT and FIRE.**"* (Matthew 3:11)

Below is a snapshot of Jesus baptizing His followers with the Spirit of God and fire.

HIS DISCIPLES

Throughout the years, much discussion and debate has taken place regarding when the disciples actually became born again. And rightfully so, people want to know at what precise moment did the disciples get saved? My approach is this, what does the Bible say how a person becomes born again?

The Bible is clear on what is necessary for a person to be saved.

*"Yet to all who **RECEIVED HIM**, to those who believed in His name, He gave the right to become children of God."* (John 1:12)

*"He then brought them and asked, 'Sirs, what must I do to be saved?' They replied, '**Believe in the Lord Jesus,** and you will be saved, you and your household.'"* (Acts 16:30-31)

"That if you confess with your mouth, 'Jesus is Lord,' and believe in your heart that God raised Him from the dead, you will be saved. For it is with your heart that you believe and are justified, and it is with your mouth that you confess and are saved." (Romans 10:9-10)

The disciples Jesus chose to follow Him got saved the same way you and I do. In fact, after His resurrection the disciples saw Jesus with their own eyes, touched Him, talked to Him and ate with Him. Without question, they confessed with their mouth that Jesus was Lord and believed in their heart that He had risen from the dead. They believed! Their conversion took place before the Holy Spirit descended upon them in the Upper Room on day of Pentecost.

In John 20:22, after Jesus' resurrection, He appears before His disciples and something special happens.

"And with that He breathed on them and said, 'Receive the Holy Spirit.'"

No doubt, at this point they believed in Jesus as the true and only Messiah, and here, Jesus exhaled and breathed on them, and they received the Spirit of God into their lives. I am convinced it was at this moment the disciples became born again. The Holy Spirit came to take up residence in them.

However, this wasn't enough; they needed more, another encounter with the Holy Spirit. So, after He breathed upon them and they received the Holy Spirit, Jesus gave them a mandate: He told them to journey to Jerusalem and wait there until they were *"**endued** with power from on high."* (Luke 24:49)

The Greek word for "endued" (v. 49) is *enduo* which means to be "arrayed or clothed." So, Jesus instructed his disciples to go to the holy city, not to be saved, but to be "clothed and arrayed" with the power of God.

Interesting isn't it?

Shortly after the disciples arrived in Jerusalem, Jesus once again appeared before them and reiterated His instructions to them:

*"**Do not leave Jerusalem**, but **WAIT** for the gift my Father promised, which you have heard me speak about. For John baptized with water, but in a few days **you will be baptized with the Holy Spirit.**"* (Acts 1:4b-5)

The Greek word for "baptism" is *baptizo*. It means to immerse, submerge, to make fully wet, soak, saturate, dip and cover. There is a reason Jesus used this word to describe their encounter with the Holy Spirit. He wanted them to be submerged in the Spirit.

Jesus further commented on what would happen to them when they were baptized, saturated with the Holy Spirit.

*"And **you shall receive power** when the Holy Spirit comes upon you."* (Acts 1:8)

Jesus knew in order for the disciples to fulfill the Great Commission, to endure the coming persecution and to do the same type ministry He did, they would need the same anointing and experience He had. And it happened just as He said it would. The disciples were gathered in the Upper Room and the Holy Spirit came upon them.

They were never the same.

*"When the Day of Pentecost had fully come, they were all with one accord in one place. And suddenly there came a sound from heaven, as of a rushing mighty wind, and it filled the whole house where they were sitting. Then there appeared to them divided tongues, as of fire, and one sat upon each of them. And **they were all filled with the Holy Spirit** and began to speak with other tongues, as the Spirit gave them utterance."* (Acts 2:1-4)

THE SAMARITANS

*"Now when the apostles who were at Jerusalem heard that Samaria had received the word of God, they sent Peter and John to them, who, when they had come down, **prayed for them that they might receive the Holy Spirit.** For as yet He had fallen upon none of them. They had only been baptized in the name of the Lord Jesus. **Then they laid hands on them, and they received the Holy Spirit."*** (Acts 8:14-17)

As mentioned earlier, before I experienced this precious baptism with the Holy Spirit, I argued vehemently that at the moment you were saved you received the fullness of God. However, the above passage obviously didn't, and doesn't, fit into my neatly organized, former theological box.

Let me explain.

The people in Acts 8 were already saved. How do I know? Philip the evangelist was commissioned to this area to preach the gospel and vast numbers of people were placing their faith in Jesus and being baptized in water. (v. 12) Yet, the text points out that Peter and John were later sent to these new converts and when they laid hands on them they received the Holy Spirit. (v. 17)

Now, being a good, loyal Baptist and staunch dispensationalist, I had an articulate explanation for these people receiving the Holy Spirit after their salvation experience. Here it goes.

I was taught and believed that these experiences with the Holy Spirit in the book of Acts were special, unique, and time-sensitive. I adhered to the party-line thinking that these and other similar encounters with the Holy Spirit only happened during the formation period of the early church. Therefore, since the people from Samaria, which represented all gentiles, were not present in the Upper Room, that Peter and John brought the power of the Holy Spirit and Pentecost to them. In other words, the people of Samaria had an "Upper Room" type encounter for all gentiles.

The problem with this logic is that it was and is based on someone's opinion. It sounded good and made my explanation of the Holy Spirit valid. I used this same reasoning to "explain away" the purpose, value and necessity of believers experiencing the baptism with the Holy Spirit. I simply told people that this was just what God had to do in the early days of the Church; it was necessary then, but not now.

However, in my search for Biblical truth, I realized that not one scripture could be used to support my *opinion*.

The more I read the book of Acts and the stories of other great men and women of God, the more I realized how wrong I was. One of my problems was that I very rarely ventured outside of my Baptist circle. I read books written by Baptists, I listened to sermons preached by Baptists, I went to a Baptist University and Baptist Seminary, plus, the articles I read were written by Baptists. My perspective on and to the Word had been from the Baptist viewpoint. And anyone who believed outside of that prism I deemed to be in error, misguided, and might I say, not trustworthy.

> I also found out that Samaria is only forty miles from Jerusalem. Surely the Holy Spirit could have traveled that far in eight years!

I soon realized while researching the validity of the baptism with the Holy Spirit that the events of Acts chapter eight occurred almost eight years after the initial coming of the Holy Spirit. This was problematic to my currently held theological positions.

I also found out that Samaria is only forty miles from Jerusalem. Surely the Holy Spirit could have traveled that far in eight years!

Let us review.

The group from Samaria became saved about eight years after the events of Pentecost, during Philip's ministry. And, at that precise moment, following the Biblical pattern, the Holy Spirit came and took up residence in their lives.

Then Peter and John came and laid hands on them and they then "received" the Holy Spirit. (v. 17) The "receiving" of the Holy Spirit came days AFTER their salvation experience.

These are two distinct events that occurred at two different times, days apart. The latter encounter is similar to what happened in Acts 2, eight years earlier.

Now, one has to ask, "Was this a one-time phenomenon, or was this indicative of a pattern developing?"

APOSTLE PAUL (Saul of Tarsus)

Saul of Tarsus was en route to Damascus. His assignment? Imprison and put to death any and all Jews who believed in the Lord Jesus Christ.

While in transit, he had a remarkable encounter with the resurrected Jesus. He was knocked down and blinded by the power of God. Most scholars concur it was at this moment Saul was saved.

After his encounter with the Lord, Saul of Tarsus was instructed to go into the city of Damascus and wait. He did not drink or eat for three days. Meanwhile, God recruited Ananias, a disciple living in Damascus, to go and minister to Saul. Ananias knew of Saul's reputation and, initially, had reservations about going, but after conversing with the Lord about this assignment, he agreed to minister to Saul.

*"And Ananias went his way and entered the house; and **laying his hands on him** he said, 'Brother Saul, the Lord*

167

Jesus, who appeared to you on the road as you came, has sent me that you may receive your sight and be filled with the Holy Spirit.'" (Acts 9:17)

Interestingly, the phrase *"filled with the Holy Spirit"* (v. 17) is the same phrase used in Acts 2:4. Also, worth noting, in Acts 1:5, Jesus called being *"filled with the Holy Spirit"* the *"baptism with the Holy Spirit."* Therefore, according to the text, Saul of Tarsus/Paul had the same experience and encounter with the Holy Spirit that the gang in the Upper Room had. Paul was unmistakably "baptized" with the Holy Spirit!

As we take a deeper look at this text, we discover two facts about this incident. First, biblical scholars would agree that the Day of Pentecost, the initial coming of the Holy Spirit, took place many years before. Secondly, Paul's remarkable experience with the Holy Spirit came a few days AFTER he was saved on the Damascus road.

Now, let me challenge your thinking by asking you two simple questions.

One, if Paul was saved on the Damascus road and received all he needed to receive at his conversion why did Jesus instruct Ananias to go lay his hands on Saul in order that He may receive his sight AND be filled with the Holy Spirit?

Two, if the experience of the day of Pentecost was to be a "one-time" event and never to be repeated again, then why was it happening again three to four years later?

You may think, as I did, "Something isn't right. The New Testament is not lining up with the way I've been taught."

I know what you are experiencing right now. I've been there and it's a helpless feeling. The truth of the matter is that this passage deals a lethal blow to the thought, "You receive all you will ever need at salvation," or, the approach, "You get it ALL at salvation."

Paul was dramatically saved three days prior and yet God had more for him.

My friend, an undeniable pattern is developing, do you see it?

CORNELIUS

Acts 10:44-46: *"While Peter was still speaking these words,* ***the Holy Spirit fell upon all those who heard the word.*** *And those of the circumcision who believed were astonished, as many as came with Peter, because the gift of the Holy Spirit had been poured out on the Gentiles also.* ***For they heard them speak with tongues and magnify God.***"

Cornelius was a Gentile who sought after God with his whole heart. God became aware of his hunger and sent Peter to his house to share with him the good news of the gospel. While Peter was declaring the wonderful news of Christ, verse forty-four tells us, *"...the Holy Spirit fell upon all those who heard the word."*

The Greek word for the phrase "fell upon" in verse forty-four is *"epipipto."* It is the same Greek word used to describe the reaction of the faithful father toward his wayward son returning home in Luke 15. We find the father "falling upon" his prodigal son, kissing, overcoming, embracing and covering him. This is exactly what happened when the Holy Spirit "fell upon" (*epipipto*) Cornelius and his household.

Cornelius and others that were present had the same type of experience the first disciples had in Acts 2. The contingent of

169

Jews present testified of this truth because they heard the Gentiles speak in tongues (v. 46), one of the manifestations of this baptism.

EPHESUS

Acts 19:1-7: *"And it happened, while Apollos was at Corinth, that Paul, having passed through the upper regions, came to Ephesus. And finding some disciples* **he said to them, 'Did you receive the Holy Spirit when you believed?'** *So they said to him, 'We have not so much as heard whether there is a Holy Spirit.' And he said to them, 'Into what then were you baptized?' So they said, 'Into John's baptism.' Then Paul said, 'John indeed baptized with a baptism of repentance, saying to the people that they should believe on Him who would come after him, that is, on Christ Jesus.' When they heard this, they were baptized in the name of the Lord Jesus.* **And when Paul had laid hands on them, the Holy Spirit came upon them, and they spoke with tongues and prophesied.** *Now the men were about twelve in all."*

I must be honest; this passage upset my Southern Baptist theological apple cart. I wasn't fully prepared for Paul's question. In the past when I would read this chapter I would quickly skim over verse two. He asked the Ephesus crowd, in verse two, *"Did you receive the Holy Spirit when you believed?"*

Here is how it unfolded.

Paul, on one of his missionary journeys, ventured into Ephesus and, while there, he found a group of John the Baptist's disciples. Paul discovered that these men were not saved (vv. 3, 4); they had not yet believed in the Lord Jesus, but only baptized in John's baptism, a baptism of repentance. Contextually, it appears they were still awaiting the coming of the Messiah. Paul recognized their lack and shared the importance of following Jesus. (v. 4) Somewhere between verses four and five these precious people became born again.

Immediately following their conversion, they were baptized with water. (v. 5) Pay close attention to what happened next. *"And when Paul had laid hands on them, the Holy Spirit came upon them and they spoke in tongues and prophesied."*

Once again, this pointed passage validates and supports the teaching that the baptism with the Holy Spirit takes place after salvation.

Let me break it down for you so you can see it.

- In verses 3 and 4, Paul discovers they are not born again.

- In verse 4, Paul teaches them about Jesus.

- In verse 5, Paul leads them to Christ.

- Also in verse 5, He water-baptizes them in the name of Jesus.

- Then in verse 6, He lays his hands on them and the Holy Spirit comes upon them.

- In the same verse, they speak in tongues.

I must ask a question. If a person receives the fullness of the Holy Spirit at salvation, then why does this text show us that the Holy Spirit came upon them *after* Paul laid his hands on them?

I don't mean to be overly redundant, but I must make the point again that this text, as well as others, clearly communicate that the baptism with the Holy Spirit is a work subsequent to salvation.

The first fifteen years of my Christian life I didn't believe in receiving the fullness of God after salvation. In my defense, I was lining up behind some well respected theologians, teachers, preachers and scholars. They were and are great men and women of God. I believed and interpreted the Bible the way they did. I submitted to the teaching and doctrine that was passed down to me as a Southern Baptist.

However, I eventually made a significant shift in what I believed. I chose to believe the way Peter, James, John and Paul believed.

My conclusion is, if it was good enough for them, then it was good enough for me. If that is how they experienced the power of God, then I was going to follow their example. If they laid hands on people to receive the baptism with the Holy Spirit, then I would do the same.

Today, I am following their pattern and guess what? I am seeing the same results they saw. People are being filled with the Holy Spirit the way it happened in Acts 2, 8, 9, 10 and 19.

If we do life and ministry the Bible way, we will get Bible results.

21

What Will Happen To Me?

People naturally want to know what will happen to them when they receive the infilling of the Holy Spirit. I know I did.

There are several opinions regarding the manifestations of the baptism with the Holy Spirit. There are some that believe you must speak in tongues as the main evidence of the baptism. They judge your experience on whether or not you manifested tongues at that moment. On the other hand, there are some who downplay the significance of tongues altogether.

I recall being at a Pentecostal Camp Meeting and the speaker asked those who wanted to be baptized with the Holy Spirit, with evidence of speaking in tongues, to come forward.

It seemed as if the entire time he kept emphasizing speaking in tongues. Not once did he mention the other results and purposes of the baptism with the Holy Spirit. Now, don't misunderstand what I am trying to say. I strongly believe every person who has experienced the baptism with the Holy Spirit should - and can - speak in tongues. I pray in tongues every day.

However, I think some people are out of balance with overemphasizing tongues and not highlighting the other valuable and necessary manifestations.

Below, I will list several of other expressions, that are equally important, that confirm you have been filled with the Holy Spirit.

HOLINESS

I do believe the most beautiful manifestation of being baptized with the Holy Spirit is holiness. The devil can counterfeit tongues, but he cannot duplicate holiness. If you have encountered the Holy Spirit in fullness then you will walk in holiness.

...the most beautiful manifestation of being baptized with the Holy Spirit is holiness.

He isn't called HOLY Spirit for nothing!

When the HOLY Spirit comes upon you, there is a shift in your life, a major refocusing. Holiness becomes a dominant

174

pursuit of yours. You don't want to sin. You want to please the Father.

We all have seen the hypocrisy; you know people who go to church and pray in tongues, but when they are out in the workplace, they are inconsistent in their walk with God and, at times, act just like an unsaved person. They use foul language, tell tasteless jokes, and display other behavior that does not honor Christ.

In my conviction, this is not right.

Therefore, being able to speak in tongues doesn't impress me (and I don't believe it impresses God), but walking pure and holy before Him and others does.

"But this is the man to whom I will look and have regard: he who is humble and of a broken and wounded spirit, and who trembles at My word and reveres my commands." (Isaiah 66:2b Amplified Bible)

"He delights not in the strength of the horse, nor does He take pleasure in the legs of man. The Lord takes pleasure in those who reverently and worshipfully fear Him, in those who hope in His mercy and loving-kindness." (Psalm 147:10-11 Amplified Bible)

"Live as children of obedience [to God]; do not conform yourselves to the evil desires [that governed you] in your former ignorance [when you did not know the requirements of the Gospel]. But as the One Who called you is holy, you yourselves also be holy in all your conduct and manner of living. For it is written, You shall be holy, for I am holy." (1 Peter 1:14-16 Amplified Bible)

Before I experienced the baptism with the Holy Spirit, I had a desire to live a holy life; however, just like many others, I struggled immensely to sustain that lifestyle before God.

After my encounter with the Holy Spirit, my desire for holiness multiplied, and today I find it easier to walk consistently in victory and purity. Before, for the most part, I was trying to live holy in the power of my flesh. I woke up each morning and said to myself, "Bless God, I'm going to live holy today even if it kills me." Well, it almost did.

To me, one of the greatest things about my encounter with the Holy Spirit that I continue to experience is the life-giving power of God that flows to me and through me.

Yes, the Holy Spirit was inside me all the time, but now John 7:37-39 is real to me. I am experiencing these *"rivers of living water"* moving through me. As a result, He has supernaturally enabled and empowered me to walk in a level of holiness I have never known before.

"On the last day, that great day of the feast, Jesus stood and cried out, saying, 'If anyone thirsts, let him come to Me and drink. He who believes in Me, as the Scripture has said, "out of his heart will flow rivers of living water."'" But this He spoke concerning the Spirit...." (John 7:37-39a)

POWER

"But you **shall RECEIVE POWER** *(ability, efficiency, and might) when the Holy Spirit has come upon you...."* (Acts 1:8 Amplified Bible)

Jesus said it! YOU WILL receive power when the Holy Spirit comes upon you. Pay close attention to the words used in the verse.

He said, *"You will receive power WHEN the Holy Spirit COMES UPON you."* He doesn't say when the Spirit comes to "dwell" in you. He says when He "comes UPON you."

All of us know the difference between "in" and "upon." For example, I place the cookies "in" the oven. Or, I place the cookies "upon" the oven. The baptism with the Holy Spirit is not the Holy Spirit coming "in" you (that happens at salvation), but rather it is the Holy Spirit coming UPON you to supernaturally empower you for service.

Again, Jesus said you will receive power when the Spirit of God comes upon you. You may ask, "Power for what?"

In short, you receive power to witness to others, overcome sin, walk in victory, to do the works of Christ, and to be the type of Christian God wants you to be.

In order to truly understand the degree of power that comes as a result of the baptism with the Holy Spirit, you need not look any further than the life of Peter the disciple. The change that took place in him was extraordinary.

Before and after pictures - don't you love them? It is always great to see someone who took control of their health and lost a lot of weight. Usually they take a picture before they start the diet in order to compare and show how much weight they have lost. This is often used as a testimony and source of encouragement to others.

My goal is not to be unfair in my description of Peter's life. I simply want show the contrast that was made in his life as a result of the baptism with the Holy Spirit - you know, the before and after "snapshots" of his ministry, *before* baptism with the Holy Spirit and the dynamic results *afterwards*.

Here are a few examples of his life **before** the day of Pentecost.

Matthew 14 - He walks on the water with Jesus, but after a few steps he takes his eyes off of Jesus and begins to sink. Jesus rebukes him for his lack of faith.

Luke 9 - Peter, James, and John are fast asleep on the mountain of transfiguration while Jesus was being visited by Moses and Elijah. When Peter wakes up, he immediately begins to talk. The first thing out of his mouth is, "It is good that I am here. Let's build three tabernacles...." Obviously, he overstates his importance and is quickly rebuked by the Father who says, "Listen to my Son...." Peter's suggestion is inappropriate, ill-timed and reveals he doesn't fully understand the Lord's mission.

Luke 22 - Jesus needs Peter to pray. It is the last few hours of Jesus' life on the earth and He asks his closest friends to accompany Him to His place of prayer. While Jesus goes to pray alone, He asks the disciples to pray together. When Jesus comes back to His friends, He finds them all asleep. Jesus no doubt is disappointed in their lack of commitment, resolve and concern. Peter can't tarry one hour in prayer on the Lord's behalf. Shortly after this event, the soldiers come to arrest Jesus. Again, Peter, not knowing the full purpose of Jesus' life and ministry, takes his knife and cuts off Malchus' ear. Jesus rebukes Peter's actions and immediately reattaches the ear.

Mark 14; Luke 22 - After they arrest Jesus, Peter follows Him at a distance. Within a short span of time, Peter goes from promising to never deny the Lord to cursing the Lord and denying ever knowing Him. It is at this point we can see the frailty and weakness of Peter.

John 21 - After watching his beloved friend die on the cross, Peter decides to go back to what he did before the Lord called him, to be a "fisher of men." Peter reopens his "fishing" enterprise.

These examples, as harsh as they may be, demonstrate the lack of power in Peter's life. However, something happened to Peter in Acts 2 that altered his entire life - he was baptized with the Holy Spirit, and the power of God came UPON him. (Acts 1:8; 2:1-4)

Notice the difference in the "after" snapshot.

Acts 2:14 - Peter stood up and preached with boldness and power the wonderful news of the resurrected Jesus. He looked the crowd square in the eyes and told them that they were responsible for Jesus' death. He spoke against their hardness of heart, their rebellion and sin. He also proclaimed Christ's infinite love for each of them. They were cut to the heart by his words and cried out in Acts 2:37, *"What shall we do?"* Peter eloquently laid before them the plan of salvation.

"And Peter said to them, 'Repent and be baptized every one of you in the name of Jesus Christ for the forgiveness of your sins, and you will receive the gift of the Holy Spirit.'" (Acts 2:38)

On this day 3,000 souls were saved!

Don't forget just a few days earlier a young girl caused him to deny the Lord. Now, here he is standing in front of thousands of people proclaiming the power of Jesus. What made the difference? Without hesitation, THE BAPTISM WITH THE HOLY SPIRIT!

Here is another "after" photo of Peter.

Acts 3 - Peter and John were going to the temple to pray and a lame man was at the gate, which is called Beautiful, asking for money. Peter looked at him and said, *"Silver and gold I do not have, but what I do have I give to you: In the name of Jesus Christ of Nazareth, rise up and walk."* (Acts 3:6)

The man immediately received strength in his legs and he got up and walked. My friend, that's power!

Acts 3:19; 4:4 - Peter continued to preach with extreme fearlessness and demanded that the people *"repent and be converted so your sins may be blotted out...."* (Acts 3:19) Over 5,000 people repented and came to the Lord. (Acts 4:4)

Acts 4 - It wasn't long, as you can imagine, until persecution came against Peter and the followers of Christ. Peter was summoned to appear before the Sanhedrin. They concluded that he should not and must not preach any more in the name of Jesus. (Acts 4:17)

Instead of denying the Lord, as he did in times past, Peter said,

"Whether it is right in the sight of God to listen to you rather than to God, you must judge, for we cannot but speak of what we have seen and heard." (Acts 4:19-20

Can you see the difference? Before, he rejected the Lord; now he is courageous and immovable, like a rock.

I could share more examples of the impressive change that took place in Peter's life, but I think you can see the full picture.

I know what you are thinking. It happened to Peter, but can it happen to me?

YES IT CAN!

It is God's desire for you to walk in the same power that Peter did. It is available to all, especially you.

BOLDNESS

One hundred twenty spirit-filled believers burst out of the Upper Room and took to the streets of Jerusalem to fearlessly tell the wonderful works of God.

Just moments before, they received the full complement of power promised them. (Acts 1:8) Now they came face to face with the same crowd that screamed, "Crucify Him!"

Were they timid? No!

Were they scared? No!

Were they retreating and running in terror? No!

They stood their ground and joyously spoke the truth about the astonishing Savior.

No man, mob, demon or Satan himself would discourage them in their efforts to evangelize the city and the world!

As noted earlier, their efforts didn't go unnoticed or unpunished by the worldly powers in charge. Both Peter and John, as well as others, suffered great persecution.

Shortly after the day of Pentecost, Peter and John were arrested, but when the authorities released them, the early disciples held a prayer meeting. (Acts 4:23-31) Take a look at what happened next.

*"And when they had prayed, the place in which they were gathered together was shaken, and **they were all filled with the Holy Spirit** and continued to **speak the word of God with boldness**."* (Acts 4:31)

When you are truly baptized with the Holy Spirit you receive a surge of confidence and boldness. One day I received a call from a dear brother who had recently experienced the baptism with the Holy Spirit and he said to me, "I have got such boldness and confidence now. I'm sharing Jesus with everybody at work."

When someone gets filled with the Spirit of God you no longer just talk about witnessing, you do it. It comes as naturally as breathing.

PASSION FOR GOD

> When someone gets filled with the Spirit of God you no longer just talk about witnessing, you do it.

Personally, for me, out of all the manifestations listed so far, this is the one I cherish the most.

Immediately after my encounter with the Holy Spirit, my passion for the Lord intensified exponentially. I went from "loving" God to being "in love with" God. There is a huge difference between the two; every spouse knows what I am talking about.

For example, you remember when you were dating your spouse. You gave her your jacket to wear; she placed your class ring on her necklace, and you both spent hours just looking at each other.

On the phone you didn't talk much; you didn't have to. You were content just listening to each other breathe. You wrote love notes, looked for every opportunity to be together, even made up knick-names for each other.

In short, you were crazy for one another and you couldn't wait to be with each other. The reason? You were IN LOVE!

When I received the baptism with the Holy Spirit, at that precise moment, my heart fluttered for God, to know Him and to love Him. I went from loving God to being in love with Him. I wanted to be with Him.

HUNGER FOR THE WORD

"I just can't get enough!" said one fellow.

Another said, "It's all making sense now."

A lady told me, "I can't wait to get home and read the Bible."

These are just a few of the comments from people who have been saved for years who recently experienced the baptism with the Holy Spirit.

Before I was impacted by the precious Holy Spirit, I had to force myself to read the Word. My discipline was my driving force.

Now, my appetite for the Word of God is my motivation. I want to know more about Him and His ways. I look forward to spending time in the Bible and listening to what He wants to say to my heart.

And, to what do I attribute this new-found hunger for the Word of God?

I attribute it to the baptism with the Holy Spirit.

Section Four

"Come And Drink"

22

Karen's Story

(It Is *Real!*)

*P*raise God for the baptism with the Holy Spirit!

Now, that statement comes from the mouth of someone who was raised an Independent Baptist in the heart of the Bible belt. (Karen Smith) I know it is not a popular statement in denominational circles, but the baptism with the Holy Spirit is not a denominational experience. It is a true, supernatural encounter and it is for every believer today.

When I encountered the baptism with the Holy Spirit, my life changed in so many ways. My understanding of the Word was enhanced as every page came alive. Revelation came more frequently and a hunger for more of Jesus grew daily. My prayer life went to another level as I prayed "'with understanding" and "prayed in the Spirit." A passion for evangelism, a desire to worship, and a realized power arose in my heart unlike ever before.

But coming to know the Holy Spirit in this way did not come easy for me. There were many obstacles, mainly my misunderstandings of the role and purpose of the Holy Spirit in a believer's life.

In fact, the Spirit of God in my life was limited to the salvation experience only. I understood His drawing me to salvation, but after that, He didn't have much responsibility in my life.

My journey to receiving the baptism with the Holy Spirit began with a trip to Atlanta one evening to hear a well-known minister speak. I was somewhat familiar with the minister only because I'd often heard him preach and teach on a local Christian radio station.

I was amazed at his knowledge of the Bible and his ability to explain the scriptures. One thing that really caught my attention about him was the power and confidence with which he articulated the text. It just seemed like he had an understanding unlike I had ever heard before. I appreciated his passion and his fellowship with the Holy Spirit. He constantly spoke of a deep love and communion he enjoyed with Him, and it caused me to wonder what his relationship with the Spirit of God was all about. The minister was Dr. Mark Rutland.

His text that evening was Acts 19:1-6. After reading the passage, Dr. Rutland began to share his personal testimony and in doing so, literally described my life at the time. He shared about his early life in ministry, a life of powerlessness, dryness, weakness, struggling, defeat, failures, and being at the end of his rope. The more I listened to his story, the more I wanted to stand up and shout, "Yes, that is my story right now!"

> The more I listened to his story, the more I wanted to stand up and shout, "Yes, that is my story right now!"

You see, at that time in my walk with the Lord, I was experiencing all the same things Dr. Rutland had experienced.

On the outside everything seemed fine, and it appeared that I "had it together." Boy, I *had* to have it together — I was a pastor's wife!

But deep on the inside, I was powerless and I couldn't figure out why. Ministry was a chore rather than a delight. My personal relationship with Jesus seemed more performance-based, constantly trying to please Him rather than enjoying a vibrant relationship of a Father and a daughter joined by a covenant.

I thought maybe I had not surrendered my all to Jesus. Perhaps, I had some hidden sin in my life that had gone unconfessed, and that was why I was powerless and often felt defeated. At times, I even questioned my salvation. I wasn't sure what it was, but I knew something was missing and I longed to realize the answer to my dilemma.

Eventually, Dr. Rutland came to the part in his sermon when he said, "Well folks, if I just described your life and your position with the Lord, let me tell you I have the answer for you."

Oh, thank God, I thought. I was finally going to hear the solution to this emptiness in my heart. I was so grateful he was not going to leave everyone present hanging, but would share the wonderful answer. Again I wanted to stand up and shout, "Tell us, sir; what do we need to do?"

Then he said, *"You must be filled with the Holy Ghost and power just as the disciples!"*

I slumped down in my seat. That was not what I wanted to hear. Surely that was not the answer! And even if it was, wasn't the baptism with the Holy Spirit a *charismatic experience?*

I was so disappointed. I thought to myself, "Well, that may be fine for some, but I am a Baptist and I do not believe in a subsequent work to salvation."

I had always believed in the work of the cross, plus or minus nothing. There was no other experience to have other than salvation. To believe there was something more than the experience of the cross was heresy, close to blasphemy.

I did not embrace his message that night, but I often wondered if Dr. Rutland was right. Was the baptism with the Holy Spirit a separate blessing after salvation? Was there such an empowering as he had presented? Was the coming of the Holy Spirit on the day of Pentecost a one-time event not to be experienced by anyone other than the early disciples, or was it a promise to all believers throughout time?

Being a left-brained person who appreciates research, understanding, and proof before I embrace something as truth, I turned to the Word to find answers for myself. I studied passages such as Acts 2:1-4, Acts 8:14-18, Acts 9:1-

17 and Acts 10:44-52, but I basically read them as I always had, remembering what I *had always been taught.*

I wanted to know the truth, so I began questioning what I had always believed. For example, what about Acts 2:1-4? Who was in the Upper Room the day the Holy Spirit fell upon them? They included Mary, the mother of Jesus, along with Peter, John, James and Matthew, just to name a few. If the baptism with the Holy Spirit was part of one's salvation, then my theology suggested those early disciples of Jesus were spiritually lost and had not embraced Jesus as their Lord.

How about Acts 8:16-17? They were saved in verse 16 and, what? Filled with the Holy Spirit in verse 17.

Then there was Acts 9:6, 17. Paul was saved in Acts 9:6 and, there it was again, filled with the Holy Spirit in Acts 9:17.

It began to occur to me that these people were saved first, then had an encounter with the infilling of the Holy Spirit. These seemed to be, although nearly simultaneous, two different events.

In addition, Acts 10 records the experience of Cornelius, a Gentile who was seeking the truths of God. God responded to his hungry heart by sending Peter to him with the Gospel message. If you follow the sequence of events closely, it is very clear what happened to Cornelius. Peter preached (10:34-43), the Holy Spirit fell on those listening (10:44), the Holy Spirit was poured out (10:45), salvation and, simultaneously, the baptism with the Holy Spirit with the evidence of speaking in tongues, and finally, they were water baptized. (10:47)

How can this be denied? There was obviously *something else* that happened to these seekers besides the experience of salvation.

Then there was Acts 19:1-5. Paul came upon a group of John's disciples some twenty years after the day of Pentecost. After some conversation, Paul realized these men had not experienced salvation in Jesus. He led them to conversion and then baptized them in water. (v. 5) In verse six, Paul *then* laid hands on them and the Holy Spirit came *upon* them, clearly two separate blessings. They spoke in tongues and prophesied upon receiving this blessing. Again, as with Cornelius, there were *two* events experienced by these disciples.

If that wasn't enough I looked at Luke 3:21-22, *"When all the people were baptized, it came to pass that Jesus also was baptized; and while He prayed, the heaven was opened. And the Holy Spirit descended in bodily form like a dove upon Him, and a voice came from heaven which said, 'You are My beloved Son; in You I am well pleased.'"* The Holy Spirit 'came upon' Jesus on the day of His water baptism, *empowering* Him for ministry on the earth as the new High Priest.

> Sadly, I was more committed to my denominational teaching than I was dedicated to finding out the truth.

I simply could not deal correctly with these passages using the understanding I had always trusted. Could it be possible what I had been taught about the baptism with the Holy Spirit was incorrect? Could I have missed something somewhere?

Sadly, I was more committed to my denominational teaching than I was dedicated to finding out the truth. I decided to push my findings aside and simply stick with what I had always understood about the baptism. I would press on the best I could regardless of the questions that lingered in my mind.

I continued to struggle and feel defeated for the next several months. Many times I felt as if I could not go on. My quiet times with the Lord were up and down. I felt no power in my prayer life. I begged God for the things I prayed about and, at times, I really didn't believe I would receive what I'd asked for anyway.

My evangelism efforts were weak, rehearsed, and dry. I spoke more from my training than from my personal experiences with the Lord.

As time passed, our first son Ty, continued to grow up, and then our second son, Ethan, was born. The pressure was really mounting by this time. I was a mom, a wife, a minister, a leader in the church, a disciple of Jesus, but I was really making a mess of things.

I grew tense, quick-tempered and I was wearing myself out.

I finally came to the end of my road.

There had to be more to this Christian life, more joy, more power, more passion, more revelation and peace.

I saw it throughout the book of Acts: the early disciples experienced growth, spiritual fruit, Kingdom power, miracles, signs, wonders, healing, and salvations.

Why was I not seeing and experiencing the same things?

What made the difference in their lives?

23

A Dream Changed Everything

Little did I know, Todd was struggling with some of the same questions I was. Where was the power of God in our lives? Where were the encounters with God?

But God knew our hearts and our desperation and He was patient with us on our journey. He saw our need for what was true. He was faithful to show Himself to us in the fullness of who He was.

Finally, on an appointed day in September years ago, Todd encountered the Holy Spirit in a most powerful way. His hunger and his willingness to surrender his theology allowed

God to work this miracle of the baptism with the Holy Spirit in his life. And *that* was the answer we had been looking for all along.

Soon after, Todd and I sat down and he began to share with me his experience. He told me of his deep desire for more of the Lord and a deeper walk with Him. He described many of the same symptoms I'd been experiencing. I was excited for him, but I feared what his full explanation would be. Was he about to tell me he'd been baptized in the Holy Spirit?

He said, "I have found the secret to what I've been searching for. I received the baptism with the Holy Spirit."

For the second time I slumped down in my chair. He was describing that *charismatic thing* that we were not supposed to consider. Didn't he know that?

Needless to say, the next few weeks in our home were stressful and tense.

Todd's life changed drastically. He was already close to the Lord, but he grew even closer and I grew jealous. He had joy and peace. He shared the gospel with others with a boldness and confidence. His love for Jesus seemed to increase more and more. He preached with power and conviction.

His messages were the same, but the presence of God rested on him and the word in a different way.

His messages were the same, but the presence of God rested on him and the word in a different way. I often heard him praying in the spirit, in the heavenly language the Lord had imparted to him. I didn't understand and I became agitated because what he had experienced was against everything we had believed.

He would tell me, "Karen, this baptism is real. It is real. And I do not want you to miss out on this. I am going to pray you through."

What I just could not seem to get beyond was all I had been formerly taught in my denomination, the doctrine and theology concerning the baptism with the Holy Spirit. I was taught this baptism was a part of one's salvation, that the Holy Spirit indwelled the believer at the time of conversion and there was no other work of the Spirit.

I was taught that the Holy Spirit came on the day of Pentecost and those present in the Upper Room were "filled" at this initial coming, but this experience was not to be had by any other believers from that day forward.

All things pertaining to the Holy Spirit - the gifts of the Spirit, signs, wonders, power and the like - stopped and passed away as the early church was established and the canon came to completion. To believe any way other than this would force me to divorce what I had always believed to be true.

I am ashamed to say my allegiance was to my former mentors and their interpretation of God's Word instead of what the Word really said. Still, I knew there had to be an answer for the powerlessness and lack of demonstration of the supernatural in my life and ministry.

I asked myself again as I had before, *"Could the answer be the baptism with the Holy Spirit?"*

In the days ahead, I continued to watch Todd as he grew closer, more confident, and stronger in the Lord. The change in his life after his baptism experience was undeniable. It seemed as if he walked two feet above the ground. There was such peace that rested on him. He had no fear of what he had encountered, regardless of those around him challenging him theologically. He had a desire to share this treasured experience with others. He never once looked back to reconsider his pursuit of the Holy Spirit.

Soon after his experience, Todd began a sermon series at our church called, *The Dynamite of God.* It was a well-documented, scriptural series of messages on the baptism with the Holy Spirit. Step by step, verse by verse, he clearly laid out a foundational explanation of the promise and the purpose of the Holy Spirit baptism in one's life.

It soon became clear to me that scripture validated the role of the Holy Spirit in the life of the believer and the Church today. His role was the same all along, for the Church then and now.

One Sunday morning during the altar call, I went forward to ask the Holy Spirit to fill me with all He had for me. Truthfully, I was still somewhat doubtful and not fully trusting God to fill me as He had filled Todd. I had not fully come to believe that God wanted to give good gifts to His children and that He would freely and generously give the Holy Spirit to me if I would only ask. (Luke 11:13)

To make a long story short, my doubt and unbelief stood in the way that morning. James 1:6-7 says if a person has doubt in his heart when he asks of God, he will not receive. That was my problem.

That evening we went to bed after a continued discussion about the baptism. There was still such struggle in my heart. I so wanted to understand and believe these wonderful things about the Holy Spirit. I wanted to believe that He had an outpouring waiting for me. I wanted to believe He would change my life as He filled me to fullness with Himself. I had seen the difference in Todd's life and in the lives of others, but I still continued to waiver.

I had been wrestling with God for months as He showed me the truths about His Spirit in the Word. Even though I had opened my heart a bit, I still was not fully convinced of the Spirit's partnership and involvement in my life. Well, we all know, you don't push against the Lord. He is patient, but when you make a decision to stand against revelation of the truth, you end up on an island by yourself.

The book of Joel says in the last days we will see visions and dream (2:28), and one night I had an unusual experience. I was not sleeping well at all and woke up several times in the night feeling an uneasiness in my spirit.

I believe I had opened a door to my life through my resistance to God's revealed truth concerning His Spirit, and the enemy was taking advantage of the opportunity.

Suddenly, I felt as if there was something or someone in our bedroom. Todd was fast asleep, but I was wide awake. I looked at the clock — it was 3:30 a.m. The best way I can describe what I felt and sensed? *Evil!*

I believe I had opened a door to my life through my resistance to God's revealed truth concerning His Spirit, and the enemy was taking advantage of the opportunity. I became afraid of what I felt and I sat up in the bed. I quickly lay back down and prayed, realizing I put myself in a compromising position by challenging the truth of God.

I had resisted Him far too long and I did not want to live another moment without His manifested presence on my life.

As soon as the sun came through the windows of our room, I quietly slipped out of the bed and went into the living room. I began to cry out to God and repent for denying His truth and the blessing of the baptism with the Holy Spirit. I asked Him to forgive me for not believing what I read in His Word. I knew I never wanted to be without His power in my life. I told the Lord I would do whatever I needed to do to have His presence continually rest upon me.

I shared with Todd what had happened the night before. I was ready to surrender and embrace the Holy Spirit. We asked some friends to come to our home one evening and we sought the Lord for the baptism. I came before the Lord that night and asked Him in faith to fill me with the Holy Spirit and power.

At that moment He filled me and just as plain as any voice I had heard, He said, "This is Me, and I am filling you." I felt ripples like water go across my whole body, very gentle ripples. I continued to yield and ask, and He continued to fill me.

I encountered the Lord that night, but I did not speak in my prayer language initially. The manifestation of that blessing came a few weeks later in a powerful way.

We had been meeting at our church for some time on Saturday nights at 10:00 for corporate prayer. Oh, what shaking prayer meetings those were! I knew the Lord had spoken to me to have a certain pastor who met with us to pray for me for the manifestation of my prayer language.

Again, as with "all things Holy Spirit," I had a mental block regarding tongues. However, at this point, I believed in the gift of the prayer language, but I simply couldn't give way to it when I prayed.

I arrived at the prayer meeting that night and found the pastor I knew was to pray for me. I explained what the Lord had told me and he agreed to pray.

He gave me sound instructions directly from scripture to build my faith. As soon as he laid hands on me, the Spirit of the Lord rose up inside me and I literally blasted the room with my prayer language! The best way I can describe it is a fire hydrant wide open! It was the most glorious and lifting thing I had ever experienced.

For the first time, my spirit-man was speaking a heavenly language directly to God. I had a new weapon in the spirit and a powerful tool for ministry.

Everything started to change. My goals changed. My attitude changed. The way I faced and prayed about circumstances changed. My finances changed. My giving changed. My passion to know Him and understand His Word exploded. Worship intensified and prayer became a joy rather than duty. I saw the truth of the Holy Spirit, His movement and work on the earth today through the church.

I believe the Lord meets us right where we are when we decide to seek Him with our whole heart. Receiving the baptism with the Holy Spirit was a journey for me, but the Lord was patient as I worked my way through His Word little by little. I realized I had embraced an incorrect doctrine and it had caused me to be so very closed to the things of the Spirit.

It wasn't until I was honest with myself, dropped my pride, and finally admitted that I could be wrong about things that I found the truth about the Holy Spirit.

In Acts 2:38-39, Peter said, *"Repent, and let every one of you be baptized in the name of Jesus Christ for the remission of sins; and you shall receive the gift of the Holy Spirit. For the promise is to you and to your children, and to all who are afar off, as many as the Lord our God will call."*

Clearly the promise of the Holy Spirit is for all generations and that promise extends to me and you.

The book of Acts was never meant to end, in the sense that it is the book that records the acts of the Holy Spirit through the church, the body of Christ. Whatever was meant for the early church is meant for the church today. That includes the baptism with the Holy Spirit, signs, wonders, miracles, healing, the spread of the Gospel, the gifts, and yes — even raising the dead!

Whatever they experienced then, we, too, can experience today.

The Holy Spirit was given to empower the early church to do the works of Jesus. He was their power then and He is our power now and nothing has changed. We need Him to fill us and empower us to do the work of the ministry and to live a victorious life.

I am grateful I finally *found the secret* to all He has for me!

24

What Must I Do?

People frequently ask me, "How can I receive the baptism with the Holy Spirit?"

One gentleman approached me and said, "What do I have to do?"

A sweet lady asked, "How do I get what you have?"

A distinguished Baptist minister came to me and said, "If it is real, then I want it." I looked at him square in the eye with a huge grin on my face and said, "My dear brother, it's real, it's real, it's real!"

The Spirit calls us to an ever-growing hunger for God and all that He has for us. People are no longer content with just "getting by" in their walk with God. Like never before, they are thirsting for that deeper life and desire to walk in the dynamite power of God. Their spirits are crying out for more.

I rejoice that people are wanting and are experiencing God and His fullness; however, there are so many more believers who need this precious baptism with the Holy Spirit, but are in churches where this is not preached or advocated.

Unless something changes, these wonderful people will remain in their current state and never enter into the blessed spirit-filled life. If that is the case, they will spend the rest of their days "trying" to make Christianity work and most of them will just "settle in" and do the best they can with what they know and have experienced.

And sadly, they will "burn out" and become frustrated in their walk with God.

Let me declare loudly and clearly, there is no reason you have to stay where you are in the Lord today. You can experience the fullness of God right now. You don't have to wait on your pastor, teacher, deacon or denomination to give you the approval. God has spoken clearly in the scriptures about His desire for His children to be empowered by the Holy Spirit.

God wants you filled with the Holy Spirit and He can fill you at this very moment. He is waiting and willing. This encounter with God can happen anywhere and at any time.

Here are some thoughts that will lead you into the fullness.

1. **YOU MUST BE SAVED**. The baptism with the Holy Spirit is for believers. If you are saved you are a candidate for the fullness of God.

2. **YOU NEED TO REPENT**. This means to turn from the wicked ways and sins in your life. Confess your sin before the Lord and ask Him to cleanse you. Be specific. Take your time here. The baptism with the Holy Spirit is not to be taken lightly. Your heart must be rendered and laid bare before Him. If you bypass this step and truly do not come clean before Him, you will never experience the infilling of the Spirit.

In addition, as I had to do, I repented that I incorrectly taught others about the baptism with the Holy Spirit. I also openly asked God to forgive me for not believing and practicing the whole Bible. Lastly, I denounced all former inaccurate teaching.

After I repented I knew I was prepared and ready to proceed in receiving the fullness of God

3. **YIELD "IT ALL" TO HIM**. Hold nothing from Him; give it all. Surrender your mind, body and spirit. Don't leave anything out. Make Him the Lord of your life, every piece of you. This is a must!

*"Do not present your members to sin as instruments for unrighteousness, but **present yourselves** to God as those who have been brought from death to life, and your members to God as instruments for righteousness."* (Romans 6:13)

4. **YOU MUST THIRST FOR HIM**. Prior to my encounter with the Holy Spirit I longed for God. I craved and cried out for His power. I was desperate and wanted all of Him. I desired

Him and nothing but Him. I chased Him and pursued Him with every ounce of energy I had.

I wholeheartedly believe you must have a thirst for God in order to be filled with the Holy Spirit. A half-hearted hunger will not do. God will not fill you if you are not desperate and hungry for Him. However, if you thirst and long for Him, He will find you and fill you!

Note what Jesus said:

*"Blessed are those who **hunger** and **thirst** for righteousness, for **they shall be filled**."* Matthew 5:6

*"On the last day, that great day of the feast, Jesus stood and cried out, saying, '**If anyone thirsts, let him come to Me and drink**. He who believes in Me, as the Scripture has said, out of his heart will flow rivers of living water.' But **this He spoke concerning the Spirit**, whom those believing in Him would receive; for the Holy Spirit was not yet given, because Jesus was not yet glorified."* (John 7:37-39)

5. **ASK IN FAITH**. Some people say, "If God wants me to have the baptism, He will give it to me. I don't need to ask for it." There is something wrong with that approach. For starters, it is not scriptural. Jesus teaches that we can and should ask for the Holy Spirit. (Luke 11:13) Also, James 4:2 says, *"You do not have because you do not ask."*

There are some who believe the way to be filled with the Holy Spirit is to yield and yield and yield some more. As mentioned above, "yielding" is a vital part of the process, but there is more. In order to receive the fullness of God YOU MUST ASK IN FAITH. And as you ask you must believe that you will receive.

206

*"If you then, being evil, know how to give good gifts to your children, **how much more** will your heavenly Father **give the Holy Spirit** to those who **ASK HIM**?"* (Luke 11:13)

I received a call from a Pentecostal believer who said she had been seeking the baptism with the Holy Spirit for years. She was concerned why she had never received.

I was, too. I said, "Dear sister, you don't have to wait and tarry for the baptism with the Holy Spirit. God wants to baptize you right now. Simply ask Him in faith, receive what He has promised and He will do it." Needless to say, she was relieved to know God's desire was for her to walk in His power immediately.

My Heavenly Father is a good Father. I don't have to beg Him for this blessed experience. It is His desire to give it willingly to you. He knows we need the power of His kingdom operating in us. Besides, God would never keep from us something He commanded us to have.

"...it is your Father's good pleasure to give you the kingdom." (John 12:32)

God takes no delight in withholding from you His power. He wants you to have it. *Ask* Him!

6. **RECEIVE HIS SPIRIT**. Many people do pray to be filled with the Spirit but don't receive. There is an action you need to take - receive!

"If anyone thirsts, let him come to me and DRINK...." (John 7:37b)

God wants us to welcome His Spirit. Open up your heart, your mouth and your spirit and drink in all that God has for you. Receive by faith the Spirit of God. Let Him flood your life with "living water."

*"Open your mouth wide and **I will fill it**."* (Psalm 81:10)

25

How Do
I Know
If I Am Ready?

Years ago, there was a young man seeking the baptism with the Holy Spirit. He had gone to every church meeting, conference and seminar on the Holy Spirit he could. Finally, he heard about an old hermit in the highlands of Scotland that had the reputation that everyone with whom he prayed instantly received the baptism with the Holy Spirit.

So the young man sold the last of his pitiful possessions and travelled all the way to Scotland to search out the old hermit. He ultimately found the hermit sitting next to a smoldering fire in a little worn-out hut near the foot of one of the most remote Munros of the Fisherfield Hills.

The young man said to the hermit, "I understand every person you pray with receives the baptism with the Holy Spirit. Is that true?"

The old hermit said, "I know a place where if you go and pray, God will fill you with the Holy Spirit."

The young man replied, "One hundred percent of the time?"

The hermit said, "Yes, one hundred percent of the time."

The young man was elated and enthusiastically responded, "Then take me there!"

The hermit replied, "Well, when do you want to go?"

"Now, right now! I want to go right now," said the young man.

Without another word the hermit plunged past the young man and ran straight into the cold outdoors. The old hermit didn't say a word, but ran as fast as he could into the night.

The young man running behind said, "Wait, wait for me! I'm coming. I want to go with you."

The hermit said nothing, not a word. The young man followed, running and running. Higher and higher they went into the dark hills. The young man's lungs were screaming for air as he ran frantically to keep up with the old hermit. He marveled that the old man could run with such nimbleness and energy. He could hardly follow him.

The young man screamed to the old man ahead, "I can't go on; is it much farther?"

Then they moved from the foothills into the shady mountains. The mountainside was so slick the young man began to fall. Now his knees were showing through his trousers. His arms were cut and his fingers were bleeding.

The young man screamed to the old man ahead, "I can't go on; is it much farther?"

The hermit said, "No, not much farther now!"

The young man screamed, "I can't last! I can't make it!"

The old man, as if to ignore the young man's desperation, started to climb a sheer cliff. It was jagged and slippery. The old man climbed the cliff with fingers so experienced. He moved with grace and ease.

The young man, filled with fear and anxiety, was barely able to move a hand or foot. He reached, grabbled and climbed from one place to the next, each inch gained in the face of terror.

Finally, he pulled himself to the top of the cliff. He rolled over on his back in total exhaustion. When he could open his eyes, he looked into the eyes of the old man and said, "I can't go another step."

The old man fell down on his knees beside him and said, "Then, this is the place."

When you get to the place where you say, "I can't make it on my own anymore, I can't take another step without Him and His power in my life," then that's the time to be filled with the Holy Spirit.

Speaking of the in-filling of the Holy Spirit in his book, *The Pursuit of Man*, A. W. Tozer writes, "It must be for the time the biggest thing in life, so acute, so intrusive as to crowd out everything else. The degree of fullness in any life accords perfectly with the intensity of true desire."[16]

If you are at this point now, then you are ready.

Below is a prayer that will lead you into the baptism with the Holy Spirit. Pray it in faith. Cry out for Him. Open wide and receive!

> Lord Jesus, I want to thank You for dying on the cross for me. I am thankful that You have saved me. You have changed my life.
>
> I ask You to forgive and cleanse my heart from all present sin. I turn my back on all known sin and rebellion in my life.
>
> Father, I am thirsty for You. I desire to know You intimately. I am hungry for You, Your holiness, purity and righteousness. I want all that You have for me. Only You can satisfy my hunger.
>
> Jesus, I know there is more to experience than what I have been experiencing in my walk with You. I know I need the baptism with the Holy Spirit. I know You desire

---

[16] A. W. Tozer, <u>The Pursuit of Man,</u> p. 133.

to give this to me. So right now, Jesus, I ask You to fill me to overflowing with the power of Your Holy Spirit. I am so hungry, so thirsty for You, Lord.

So now, Lord, I humbly ask You to baptize me now in the Holy Spirit. Come, come, Holy Spirit! Fill me, in Jesus' name! By faith, I receive the baptism with the Holy Spirit.

Thank You Father for filling me. Thank You, Lord, for the power of the Spirit that is coming upon me. Thank You, Lord, for baptizing me with the Holy Spirit.

In the name of Jesus — RECEIVE THE HOLY SPIRIT!

At this moment, begin to praise Him and, out of your belly, let your new prayer language (tongues) come forth.

Give voice to the new language.

Release it now, in Jesus' name!

26

A Message To Pastors

Not long after my supernatural encounter with the Holy Spirit, I had a lunch meeting with a fellow Baptist pastor. To my surprise he told me that 20 years earlier he, too, had experienced the baptism with the Holy Spirit. I was overjoyed to find another Baptist pastor who had the same encounter I did.

I enthusiastically asked him if he had ever shared the great news with his congregation. He replied, "No."

To be honest, his response startled me, momentarily. I stopped eating and just stared at him with angry eyes. I know he must have wondered why I was just looking at him motionless. Every part of me went on pause as my thoughts tried to catch up with me. I couldn't believe what I heard him say. Then he gave me his reason: "I didn't want to cause trouble in the church."

On the surface that sounded noble, honorable and respectable. However, the more I thought about what he just said, the angrier I became, right there in the restaurant. Honestly, I wanted to stab him with my fork! (Just kidding!) But, I was mad.

Needless to say, I lost all respect for him.

Why?

He had the most precious encounter with the Holy Spirit a human can have. He experienced the Holy Spirit in fullness and tasted heavenly power, and yet he refused to tell the people he was called to lead.

It's one thing not to experience it and, therefore, not teach about it, but to have that blessed experience and keep it to yourself!

I guess he was more interested in "staying the course" than going on with God. He had the key to power and victory, but refused to lead his people to these greener pastures. Evidently, fear kept him from speaking the truth. Perhaps he was afraid of losing his job, security and comfort. May God have mercy!

Listen to me, pastors, the baptism with the Holy Spirit is too life-changing not to share it with your people. Your flock needs to be told the truth, the whole truth. They are looking for that deeper life. They are starving for more of God. Don't hold back; preach the Word! *All* of it!!!

Many pastors worry about the problems it may cause if they preach on the fullness of God. I get it. I understand your concerns. Let me assure you, it will cause problems. The truth, when preached with power, usually causes a disturbance.

Regardless of the consequences, you are called to represent God and His Word to the people He has appointed you to lead. God expects you to preach the whole counsel of God. God will see you through any reaction the people may have. He is faithful; trust Him.

Perhaps others of you are thinking, "I don't want to get fired." Or, "I'm afraid of what the deacons will say," or "I am concerned who will leave the church."

Again, I understand how you feel, and these are honest thoughts and reactions. There is no question that people will not see the Word the way you do, especially if you are in a denominational church. People will leave your church and it's possible you may get fired.

Be courageous! Show yourself worthy of the ministry. Don't retreat, but rise to the challenge and stand on the Word. Be willing to pay whatever the cost may be.

However, this is the moment of truth and a Kingdom opportunity for you. Be courageous! Show yourself worthy of the ministry. Don't retreat, but rise to the challenge and stand on the Word. Be willing to pay whatever the cost may be. Your primary role is to preach His word and to please Him above all things.

It has been said, "If you don't preach the truth because you are worried about what it will cost you, you are not a preacher or prophet, you are a puppet!"

Wow, that statement is strong!

Let me encourage you. Don't allow people, fear, circumstances and money to dictate what you preach. If you do, quit preaching.

If we pastors will not preach the truth because of fear of the aftermath or fallout, then we are no better than Judas Iscariot! He had a price, too! His was thirty pieces of silver.

Pastor, don't have a price! Obey God and He will take care of you and your family.

In these precarious last days, God is looking for men and women who will truly be men and women of God. He is looking for the Elijahs who will confront the religious system of cold dispensationalism.

Who among us is willing to stand up and proclaim that God is real and His power is available?

God's eyes are roaming the earth; may He not pass over you due to your fear and need for security!

My dear friend, do whatever you have to do to have His favor and power on your life.

"For the eyes of the Lord run to and fro throughout the whole earth, to show Himself strong on behalf of those whose heart is loyal to Him...." (2 Chronicles 16:9)

We all know that David was favored by the Lord. Have you ever thought about why?

Obviously, there was something about David that attracted God to him. There was a peculiar element of his life that God really liked.

Again, have you ever wondered what that was? I have, and I think I found it.

I discovered why God said that David was *"a man after my own heart."* The answer is in Acts 13:22.

Before I give you the reason I want you to take note of something significant. Take a look at the verse again. Don't miss the first four words.

"I HAVE FOUND DAVID...."

This tells me God was searching for someone. Not just anyone, but He was searching for a particular type of leader. Someone who would obey Him no matter what! A person who would not be afraid to make tough decisions and who had the fortitude to endure when the going gets rough! Someone that could bravely face lions, bears and GIANTS when others cowered in fear!

Here is why "David was a man after God's own heart:"

David would do ALL of HIS WILL.

"I have found David the son of Jesse, a man after My own heart, who will do all My will...." (Acts 13:22)

Not *part* of it, not *most* of it, not *the safe part* of it, not just the *convenient part* of it, but *ALL* of IT!

The New Living Translation says it this way:

"I have found David son of Jesse, a man after my own heart. ***He will do everything I want him to do."***

This is why God was attracted to David!

God knew that no matter what He asked David to do, no matter what He required of Him, David would obey and do it!

I wonder if God feels the same way about me.

Does God know that no matter what He asks, regardless of the cost or sacrifice, I will obey?

How about you? Can He say, "He/she will do everything I want him/her to do?"

Pastor, the hour is late, the world is in shambles and the contemporary church is mostly impotent.

Don't compromise! Be strong!

Preach the whole counsel of God!

Operate in the fullness of His power and let Him use you mightily during this end-time harvest. One day, you will be glad you did.

27

"You Ain't Seen Nothing Yet!"

I am truly saddened because many believers are not going to experience the fullness of God in their lives.

Personal preferences and denominational teachings will be placed above the Word of God.

Apprehensions and fears will keep many from this precious baptism.

The end result will be that the Kingdom of God suffers and lives will lack power.

My heart breaks because many people are settling for less than God's best.

Did you know that God will allow you to go without the Holy Spirit's fullness in your life as long as you think you don't need Him?

I have discovered that **God does not squander His blessings on those who feel no need for them**.

Many believers who lead respectable lives will never receive the fullness of the Holy Spirit simply because they feel no need for it. They are satisfied without this blessing, and God leaves it that way.

This was true in my life. For years, I wasn't open to the baptism with the Holy Spirit.

God simply said, "Okay, if that is the way you want it, then that is the way it is going to be." The good news is, God in His infinite goodness makes available the spirit-filled life to everyone.

However, it is up to us whether or not we partake of it. He lets us make that decision.

Many years ago, there was a trailer park in Marietta, Georgia, that was called the "Abundant Living Trailer Park."

The sign advertising the community read, "UNTIL YOU STEP INSIDE, YOU AIN'T SEEN NOTHING YET!"

The day I walked into a Pentecostal prayer meeting, I stepped inside God's "Abundant Living…."

My life has never been the same since that day. I'm glad I took a step of faith and decided to go see what was inside.

It is true: until you do, **YOU AIN'T SEEN NOTHING YET!**

# # #

Other Powerful Books And Resources By Todd Smith:

HE SAT DOWN

This is a must have. It is provocative and revolutionary. For too long, the Church has been waiting for Jesus to do everything. The Bible says, "HE SAT DOWN." God will never do what He has left for His Church/children to do. Todd dares you to read this book. You will never be the same. Will you stand up?

Right now in heaven, Jesus is seated. His work on the earth today has to be done by us. Will you stand up?

www.kingdomready.tv

40 DAYS - A Journey Toward a Deeper Relationship with Christ

This book is a lot of fun. It is an interactive devotional book designed to help you DEVELOP consistency in your private devotional time.

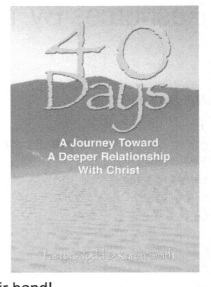

Most Christians struggle with being consistent in their quiet time with the Lord. This resource will get you in the Word and help develop your faith.

Plus, every new believer should start their new journey with Christ with this book in their hand!

"40 DAYS" is a premier tool that will help you mature in your relationship with Jesus.

www.kingdomready.tv

Encounter...WORD POWER!

This is one of everyone's favorites. It is packed with power! Over 360 topical scriptures on such topics as, Leadership, Parenting, Marriage, Temptation, etc.

In addition, over one hundred twenty quotes from various leaders highlight each topic. It's enjoyable and inspirational. And, it makes a great gift for anyone.

www.kingdomready.tv

10 THINGS EVERY PASTOR NEEDS TO KNOW

(Available in digital format only)

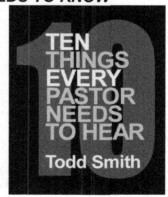

I wish someone had told me the truth about pastoring. It has been a joy to lead people, but it also has been difficult. Only one in ten pastors makes it to retirement; ninety percent leave the ministry. This short book will encourage and equip pastors to finish strong.

Get a copy for your pastor!

To Order VISIT US at www.kingdomready.tv

Made in the USA
Middletown, DE
18 May 2021

39939450R00126